D0611479

Post Scripts

Vincent Kaufmann

Post Scripts
the writer's workshop

Translated by Deborah Treisman

Harvard University Press

Cambridge, Massachusetts, and London, England   1994

Copyright © 1994 by the President and Fellows
of Harvard College
All rights reserved
Printed in the United States of America

Originally published as *L'équivoque épistolaire,* © 1990
by Les Editions de Minuit

This book is printed on acid-free paper, and its binding
materials have been chosen for strength and durability.

Library of Congress Cataloging-in-Publication Data
Kaufmann, Vincent, 1955-
[L'équivoque épistolaire. French]
Post scripts : the writer's workshop / Vincent Kaufmann;
translated by Deborah Treisman.
        p.   cm.
Translation of: L'équivoque épistolaire.
Includes bibliographical references and index.
ISBN 0–674–69330–2
1. French letters—History and criticism.   2. Authors,
French—Correspondence—History and criticism.
3. French prose literature—History and criticism.
4. German prose literature—History and criticism.
5. German letters—History and criticism.   6. Letter-
writing, German—History.   7. Letter-writing, French—
History.   8. Psychoanalysis and literature.   9. Modernism
(Literature).   I. Title.
PQ611.K3814   1994
846.009—dc20   93–34066
CIP

Designed by Gwen Frankfeldt

Contents

Post Scripts

Reading in Bed

"How do you read?" a psychoanalyst once asked me, after a talk I gave on Rilke's correspondence. The question showed methodological concern, but was well-meant, conspiratorial, and was intended to make me admit what my reading method owed to psychoanalysis. Without thinking, I short-circuited the theoretical debate my companion wanted by answering that I always read "lying down." He seemed, like me, rather surprised by the answer but also satisfied, more satisfied probably than if I had launched into a technical explanation. I was dealing with a real psychoanalyst, I thought.

In fact through what was, when it comes down to it, a misunderstanding, everything had somehow already been said. First because the conversation was the result of a misunderstanding and psychoanalysis depends fundamentally on the existence of misunderstandings—which are just as important as understandings. And, second, because answering "lying down" to a psychoanalyst whose question was basically theoretical would remind him of his patients who, lying on his couch, are not in the least concerned with methodology. It would suggest that reading a text from an analytical point of view requires the reader to occupy not only the position of the analyst—from whom he borrows a certain assumed knowledge—but also the position of the patient being analyzed, of the one who is there to express himself in words. Valéry once said that the poem listens to its reader. We could say more generally that reading a text in an analytical way, observing its gaps and repetitions, makes us its "analyst" but also puts us in a position to *be* analyzed or "spoken" by the text—and for this second possibility to occur, I think, we have to read lying down.

In order to create misunderstanding, you need a kind of reading that is both concentrated and distracted. You must learn to avoid libraries, where you can't lie down; you must give your body the chance to forget itself, which it doesn't have on a chair or at a desk. When you read sitting, the text is opposite, drawing you into a dialogue. But to understand or imagine the unspoken subtext of a text, you need to avoid a face-to-face confrontation. You have to dodge its direct appeals and distance yourself, so as not to answer only what it wants you to answer. You need a capacity not for sympathy and dialogue, but for impassivity and absence. You must always read from the position of a third party, a dead third party perhaps—the position that Lacan assigns to the analyst.[1] It is easiest to do this lying down because, prostrate, you can forget yourself and disappear. (Lying down is the most popular position for disappearing, if not permanently, then at least into sleep, and there are few experiences more deeply satisfying than falling asleep while reading.)

That is about all I can say about the analytical dimension of my reading "method," which is more a constraint than a theoretical choice. I sometimes think that it is simply a result of my inability to read when I am *not* lying down. Maybe this inability has limited my literary interests, or prevented me from becoming the literary historian I always dreamed of being. Even more seriously, maybe my taste for the prone position actually inspired me to write this book, which is dedicated to the letters of a number of writers (Kafka, Flaubert, Proust, Rilke, Baudelaire, Mallarmé, Artaud, Valéry, and Gide, in order of appearance). If it is conceivable for the specialist of a particular writer to read his or her entire correspondence sitting up—as a primary biographical document, say—it is virtually impossible to read the complete correspondence of several writers without lying down. There is, first of all, the boredom that this genre can provoke. How can you get through Baudelaire's interminable requests for money, Proust's no less interminable health bulletins, or Rilke's domestic worries, except by preparing yourself for the sleep to come and by offering it the least resistance in order to concentrate all the more when you wake up?

Then there is the fact that these letters constitute, more than most truly literary texts, an *analytical space*. (Some writers, like Proust, compose their letters in bed, while others, like Kafka, write them at night instead of sleeping or dreaming.) A psychoanalytical treatment and an epistolary exchange have several elements in common—the most significant being between the person to whom one writes, often over a period of years, and the analyst to whom one speaks, also over a period of several years. Both figures have an ambiguous or equivocal status. They are there without being *there*. The first cannot respond immediately and the second stops herself from doing so. They exist within a "depragmatized" discourse, floating between reality and fiction (or fantasy). Like the analyst, the correspondent exists as a listener. But inasmuch as she maintains a necessary silence, the speech ostensibly addressed to her drifts into the essential irresponsibility that is also necessary for desire to surface. By moving into the shadow, your correspondent gives free reign to your imagination, to narcissism, to the mirror effect; she teaches you to enjoy the sound of your own voice. By remaining there, though, she also leads you to a point where the imagination exhausts itself; working in a void, it loses solidity, becomes removed from itself, as if watching an image of itself. Behind the requests entrusted to the mailman, in the spaces between the lines, lies something akin to truth, and to desire.

There is nothing more tedious in a writer's work than his correspondence: your arms give way under the weight of its repetitious pages and it must be propped up, against the pillows. But it is precisely in these repetitions, where something refuses to be properly expressed to someone else, where it resists the passage into words, that the act of writing letters constitutes a form of analysis; and this is also why so many writers have been seduced by letters. They are of course not the only ones to write letters, but one can't help noticing that a surprisingly large number of them have devoted themselves wholly to letters, almost as others give themselves over to drugs. The letters I will examine here reveal several writers who are unquestionably fascinated by the silence or secrecy of their communications, by the methods they discover to *distance* the other to whom they speak or write. Their letters are secondary to this fascination and, as such, are an entry into wild psychoanalysis.

Usually we see letters as a means of drawing closer to the other, of communicating. But perhaps what we experience is really only a division or estrangement—a distancing that allows us also to stand back from ourselves, to witness our own disappearance. There is something fundamentally ambiguous in the epistolary impulse, and its development leads to the very frontiers of poetry. Although letters seem to facilitate communication and proximity, they produce instead a distance in which writers find the chance to become writers. If the letter writer wanted to communicate, he would not write at all. This ideal possibility not to communicate is, in my opinion, the reason why so many writers undertake voluminous and relentless correspondence, untiringly calling on others only to dismiss them again.

Letters give the writer a chance to avoid dialogue. Such is the hypothesis of this book, where I discuss a number of writers' correspondences as so many workshops where noncommunication is constructed and carefully maintained. In other words, I have not written a history of epistolary writing, or a poetics of letters, or a study of a genre that clearly extends far beyond the literary sphere. If I absolutely had to answer not "How do you read?" but "*Why* do you read that way?" I would describe this work as my theoretical, and analytical, contribution to the long debate over the reception of the literary text.

To the ideal or implicit readers assumed by the aesthetics of reception,[2] and to the readers with whom, whether in accordance with

4

Bakhtin or not, one maintains a dialogic relationship, I propose to add another kind of reader: not a partner in dialogue, and even less a partner in a trivia game (all too often the only game that specialists in this field know how to play), but a desired reader who is fundamentally absent. One of the primary interests of the correspondence I discuss here is the writer's desire to make the other disappear—to the point of being willing to disappear himself. From the Lacanian perspective, one could say that what characterizes the literary text is the ability to address, above and beyond the imaginary other (who is always similar to oneself), an Other who is the cause or source of desire. It is the ability to address (according to the formula I will elaborate in relation to Kafka) no one, but no one *in particular.*

In short, I want to play the epistolary against the dialogic and the hermeneutic. It may not seem a particularly timely debate, but I am not convinced that it isn't—especially in an academic context that places so much importance on fixed cultural identities and seems generally uninterested in the disappearance of the reader or the writer. Evidently, impassivity and irresponsibility are not highly valued these days.

A Return to the Biographical

Perhaps I need to specify that neither the irresponsibility nor the impassivity I substitute for critical reasoning represents in any way a "textual" bias. I am not particularly comfortable with "the work speaks for itself" or "the death of the author," credos for which Blanchot, Barthes, and Foucault have fought so hard with all the piety and evangelism required in these matters. Instead of bowing to the thanatographic myths that continue to form the ultimate legitimacy of literary discourse, the analysis I plan in this book will be a reactualization of the biographical question—more precisely, I will attempt to show that the thanatographic is simply a variant or flipside of the biographical. Like many of my contemporaries, in the past I learned scrupulously to ignore the lives of the writers I was interested in. The death of the author, that literary spoilsport, had just been decreed: his presence was not only superfluous but even an impediment to readings that aspired to any kind of rigor. There was a cold war between the life and the work; the borders were closed and those willing to cross them were rare.

Imagine my confusion when I found, in Kafka, Flaubert, Artaud, and others, the marked personality of the letter writer. I couldn't help becoming attached to it, but without ever being sure whether I was dealing with a living being or a "writing" being. Did the letter writer's often frenzied activity bite into the time he was given to live or into the time he owed to literature? Was it legitimate to be interested in writers' letters, fragments of life overwritten for some or texts not textual enough for others? From whichever side of the border one approached him, the letter writer seemed like an infectious renegade and threatened to transform those who took an interest in his situation into double agents. Luckily, detente took its course, the cold war is over (at least in the domain of literary studies, *this* one is over), and the renegades are tolerated now. It is lucky for the letter writer because I am still not sure which side of the border he comes from—and am no worse off not knowing it. In fact, he always seems to be coming from the *other* side or from the border itself. His milieu of choice is a minefield, a no-man's-land hidden between text and life: an elusive zone leading from what he is to what he writes, where life becomes a work and the work becomes a life. The epistolary allows for the theory that, no matter how far back we look, the writer's life has already been textualized, a life lived in letters, and that the work is never more than a kind of schematization, a shape given to the life. It makes us reassess the literary phenomenon as a systematization of biography, given of course that we acknowledge the necessarily graphic or written dimension of biography.

Such is, in any case, the intuition I will try to prove correct here. Letters are a passage between the lived and the written, independent of their potential aesthetic value. They position and keep the writer's life within the literary sphere. The letter writer is thus the infamous missing link between the person and the work, the yeti of literature. Such a claim may seem peremptory or, at best, naive, and I am certainly not the first to try to describe the link. In every critic there is doubtless a geneticist, an abominable-snowman hunter, struggling to get out. And no one is particularly convinced by the abominable-snowman theory: he may never have existed outside the human imagination. But this is exactly why I place the letter writer in that category. The abominable correspondent whose tracks I plan to follow has little more basis in science than his Tibetan counterpart. He has descended from a lineage whose imaginary quality I accept—I would rather run the risk of seeing him melt into the landscape from time to time than see him transformed into a common primate through all those academic attempts to explain his existence.

"The yeti of literature": this is also a way of saying that, as the missing link between life and art, the letter writer is entrenched in myth and, more specifically, in the myth of a separate—sacred—"literary space" espoused by Blanchot.[3] He comes from this myth or, more precisely, comes back from this myth, which also indicates, I hope, that he leaves it behind him. Maurice Blanchot was, to my knowledge, the first to note that *A la recherche du temps perdu* was the result of Proust's epistolary apprenticeship. But it was a theory he did not linger over or try to document; not, of course, because he was unable to but because the myth, or *his* myth, of writing wanted it that way. To give full credibility to the idea of an "essential solitude," or a radically separate literary space that has nothing to do with the "unrefined word" Mallarmé talks about,[4] one must both assume an entry into writing and avoid discussing the specifics or the singularity of this entry—it will always be the point at which writing becomes sacred, an invisible and indescribable meeting place between the profanity of "unrefined words" and the sanctity of "essential words." This is why presenting the figure (or multiple figures) of the letter writer, on a stage that is the frontier of literature, de-sanctifies the literary space, without destroying its specificity. After all, it must be possible to turn that space into something other than the myth by which certain contemporary critics identify writing itself. Myth by definition resists singularity, or subjectivity, and does so even more if it is the myth of a form of writing that is radically withdrawn and unpresentable. It is hardly compatible with the multiplication of figures and representations that make up the epistolary world, at the junction of life and work.

Having, perhaps, evolved from a sentence of Blanchot's, my book has no ambition other than to leave its origins behind. The "disappearance of the artist" in Mallarmé, Flaubert, or Proust, which is undeniably *at work* in their correspondence, is no longer quite the same when, instead of simply declaring it, one follows its traces in the writer's *life* through his letters. The death of a writer becomes something other than a perfectly rhetorical (and evangelical) justification of the literary discourse when it is embodied in his life: the thanatographic must be read and understood, not in philosophical terms but in biographical terms. After all, not everyone can experience the author's death. It must be paid for with your self and even, as the correspondence discussed here shows so clearly, with the other. It requires not only a taste or a gift for self-sacrifice, but also a capacity for becoming inhuman, sometimes even cruel or monstrous, as the real abominable snowman would likely be. And letters are unquestionably the perfect place to watch the "inhumanization" that so often characterizes the writer—who does not necessarily have better intentions than the nonwriting segment of humanity. The writer is neither a philosophical abstraction nor a saint, and what he does is far from sacred. This should not in any way diminish the interest or admiration we can feel for him or his works; nor should it lead us to judge him. On the contrary, it makes him all the more exciting and, in any case, more real.

Madame de Sévigné's Proustian Side

Although it has become paradoxical in my mind, the reference to Blanchot will probably still seem a sign of attachment to the so-called modernist period of European literary history. "My" authors overlap with Blanchot's and have often been at the center of the most striking propositions and theoretical debates of the last quarter century. You might expect this choice of subject matter to limit the scope of my discussion of the epistolary genre, which would have meaning only within the framework of modernism. Then you would only have to return to romanticism, or better to classicism and the traditional golden age of letters that was the eighteenth century, in order to challenge my theory, to show that nothing was as it became later.

I would like to respond to this hypothetical restriction by worsening my own case. Even in the modernist period of literature, there is no shortage of exceptions and counter-examples to indicate other uses and functions of writers' letters, beyond the role of missing link suggested above. I will not even mention the letters I have not read, whether for lack of time or interest or simply because they are inaccessible or unpublished. But think of the letters from Africa of a writer as undeniably modernist as Rimbaud. It is difficult to think of those letters as a literary workshop, since they come *after* the work. Or take the correspondence between Francis Ponge and Jean Paulhan, which suggests a completely different kind of writing workshop, rooted more in friendship, complicity, and cooperation than in a desire for distance.[5] Or, in a slightly less modernist register, think of Sartre's letters to Simone de Beauvoir, in which one can see something more like a bashful or secret stage of Sartrian autobiography than an experimentation with absence and desire.[6]

And I will risk worsening my case a second time. Even among the writers I have chosen to discuss here, there are counter-examples, notably Valéry and Rilke, who also refused to admit that one always writes blindly to a blind man, without an identifiable correspondent, and who became involved in letter writing precisely for this reason. Inversely, and this time in my defense, I will say that I am not convinced that cases like those of Rimbaud or Ponge are so different from the ones I discuss. After all, living in Africa is a distancing experience for Rimbaud, and it is easy to find the traces of transference—hence desire—in Ponge's relationship to Paulhan considering that Ponge was the first to point them out.[7]

This leads me to propose two hypotheses. First, the modernist epoch—at least as I know it—is made up of exceptions, counterexamples, and singularities. In fact, it seems so heterogeneous that I wonder whether modernism could exist as anything other than a period of singularization—and the world of difference that exists between Flaubert and Rilke or Artaud will not convince me otherwise. Second, what characterizes a writer's correspondence (and what makes it literature) is that it is always brought about by his existence as a writer, even after the fact, as in Rimbaud's case. Of course not all writers write writers' letters and, inversely, writers are not the only ones to write writers' letters. Fundamentally, though, a writer's correspondence exists only where it can form a link between life and work. It is up to each reader, beginning with the examples given here, to discover this link: each writer's correspondence is played out in a specific montage with a specific work. Above and beyond the considerations of time, knowledge, and space, my choice of writers reflects only my own preference, which tends toward writers whose work turns on the paradoxical destination of speech when it passes into writing, and toward those who are the most sensitive to the possibilities for a rupture of discourse in writing. What Baudelaire, Flaubert, Mallarmé, Proust, Rilke, and Kafka share is not a cultural or historical context, but a taste for distance and perversion.

I am even less convinced of the existence of modernism—or at least of the modernist character of the epistolary theory developed here— since it is possible to find many of the same traits in writers of other eras. The modern era is certainly not the first to experiment with desire as a poetic force and it has no monopoly on perversion. Proust was the first to see that there was something of Dostoevsky in Madame de Sévigné's letters. Today we see more of a Proustian (mother-and-son) quality in them; the historical context of the emergence of private writing aside, we are struck most by the possessive character of the mother-daughter relationship. Madame de Grignan pays a high price for her mother's entry into the ranks of writers, and Madame de Sévigné is also aware of her letters' shortcomings: "I am killing you with the length of my letters."[8] Her letters are overwhelming, deadly, and the daughter survives her by only nine years. Like the letters that pass between Proust and his mother, they force the untiring discussion of a tyrannical passion onto the other. They are born of desire, of a speech Madame de Sévigné qualified as vain three centuries before Blanchot: "This exchange is thus what's known as vain words, which have no other goal than to make you, my darling, see that my feelings for you would be perfectly happy if God didn't allow them to be mixed with the unhappiness of not having you anymore, and to persuade you also that all that comes to me from you or by you goes straight to my heart."[9] If Madame de Sévigné is a classic, she owes it perhaps less to her rhetorical talents than to her ability to make rhetoric useless, to build it, in Lacan's formula, with a speech full of the lack of desire. Her correspondence is, accordingly, not all that different from that of the modernists.

Nor is there a reason to stop at the Proustian qualities of Madame de Sévigné. Without even raising the difficult question of authenticity, we could also discuss the Kafkaesque (or Flaubert-like, given the latter's desire to become a hermit or saint) side to the letters of Abelard and Heloise; cast Fulbert as a slightly more offensive (given the era) version of Felice Bauer's father, and look at Abelard's castration as a variation on Kafka's tuberculosis. Heloise and Abelard's story is, like Kafka's, an evasion of marriage: distance is maintained, sexuality is impossible (as the castrator Fulbert understands so well), and desire is epistolary. Rousseau, of course, knew this and made their story into an epistolary novel. In Rousseau's writing in general, though, the Kafkaesque quality seems less interesting to me than the resemblance to Artaud's letters—Rousseau is Artaud's ancestor in paranoia. I am thinking specifically of the claim, explicit at the beginning of the *Confessions*, of absolute singularity and authenticity, which is also at the heart of Artaud's famous letters to Jacques Rivière, director of the *Nouvelle revue française*. Also, Artaud enters literature through his correspondence with Rivière, just as the *Confessions* has an epistolary prehistory. (It is generally acknowledged that the *Confessions* is based on Rousseau's letters to Malesherbes, whose censoring function is not unlike Rivière's relationship to Artaud.)

From Rousseau to Artaud, the conditions for the emergence and destination of writing change far less than is often believed. Some say that Rousseau was the first modernist—which perhaps extends the category too far; I'm not sure that things were so very different for Montaigne, for example, who wrote his *Essays* for the late Raimond Sebond, his old friend and conversant,[10] and whose melancholy pose is not unlike that of Flaubert, permanently in mourning for his sister Caroline, or Proust, whose *Recherche du temps perdu* has been called a long postscript—containing all the things he was unable to tell his mother when she was alive. Critics have also noted Pascal's debt to the epistolary mode, particularly his technique of fragmenting the speaking locations, which comes into his work here and there as an experiment with distance.[11] Thanks to letters, Blaise Pascal becomes Roland Barthes; he makes himself protean, atopical, even polyphonic. The epistolary genre carries him too into the modernist period. Closer to our own time, there are numerous romantic correspondences that seem to be workshops for fiction. Alfred de Musset in his letters presents himself literally as his own hero, Perdican, who has just broken things off with Camille (more likely, George Sand). And Balzac's letters, full of plot and complicated romantic intrigue, form the antechamber for *La comédie humaine*, a human comedy that pre-dates the literary version.

I am not trying to deny that all the instances mentioned come from different eras, cultures, and historical contexts, requiring as many specific descriptions and much decoding. But too much history or culture can also, as Lacan says of the imaginary, block the truly literary dynamic of a writer's correspondence. Behind the instituted discursive practices, analyzable in historical terms, there are Madame de Sévigné's vain words, in almost infinite number. Behind the rhetorical smokescreen, there are the machinations, plots, and inventions of desire, which knows so well how to feed on the misrepresentations and obstacles that it imposes on itself or are imposed by others. From Abelard through Sade to Artaud, the epistolary genre follows the same routes to literature. And it is preferably read lying down.

chapter one

Destination: Distance

Just Out of Reach

He lives in Prague, she lives in Berlin, but no matter: their letters fill him with hope and expectation. He feels as if there is no distance between them, no border, no limit. They confide in each other, they are carried away, swept into a dizzying intimacy that overcomes every obstacle. Through letters, their pleasure is immediate. They become almost tangible to each other, as if only just out of reach.

There is something magical about letters. They make distant reunions seem imminent. They satisfy the desires that they themselves create—of which they are, indeed, the only source. If Franz Kafka fell for Felice Bauer, it was due much less to their one meeting—at a party given by the parents of his friend Max Brod—than to the fact that, after some hesitation, she decided to answer his first letters. The postage stamp is always Kafka's romantic trademark. Confidences, intimacy, declarations of love that become more and more exalted, engagement: everything happens through the mail. It is only in letters that Franz really meets Felice. During the evening at the Brods', he was struck most by her emptiness and insignificance, described a few days later in his *Diary:* "Bony, empty face that wore its emptiness openly." Later, when explaining to Felice what had attracted him to her, he speaks of indifference: "At first sight I was quite definitely and incomprehensibly indifferent to you, and for this reason you may have seemed familiar" (December 2, 1912).

For letters to work their unifying magic, Felice had to begin as a cipher, familiar but neither seductive nor moving: a sketch that Kafka could later fill in and enlarge to a full portrait, which he works relentlessly to complete. And in order for this epistolary possession to take place, Kafka has to have, from the beginning, a kind of indifference to reality. In his letters the real Felice is overwhelmed, almost violated, and, for the minor crime of insignificance, deprived of her own identity, of her daily life (and of her time—a significant loss when one considers how much of it she had to spend answering her strange suitor). The tie created defies reality, and is supported only by the binding force that Kafka attributes to the written word.

As far as epistolary attachments go, I should add, this is not Kafka's first attempt. Barely a month before he met Felice Bauer, his attention was directed to the young Margaret Kirchner, daughter of the caretaker of Goethe's house at Weimar. In a letter to Max Brod, he copied out a postcard she had sent him, adding: "Above all consider that these lines are literature from beginning to end. For if I am not, in her eyes, unpleasant, I am at any rate of no more importance to her than a pot. But then why does she write as I would wish it? Do you suppose it is true that one can attach girls to oneself by writing?" (July 13, 1912). Again a matter of indifference, and in this case perhaps too well recognized as such for the correspondence to take—as if the artificiality of the situation were too obvious; it corresponds to nothing in reality. But it is just as difficult to speak of a "correspondence" in the relationship between Kafka and Felice. Kafka destroyed all of her letters, and we see only his side of the affair.

Eighteen months after their first meeting, Kafka and Felice still seem just out of each other's reach. Three days before finally agreeing to an engagement, Kafka sends Felice another unenthusiastic assessment of their relationship: "But look, for more than 18 months we have been running to meet each other, yet seemed, before the first month was up, already to be almost breast to breast. But now, after all this time, after so much running, we are still so very far apart" (April 9, 1914). The epistolary magic has gone, the enchantment has missed its target. It is like the courier in "An Imperial Message": he is strong, swift, untiring. The emperor on his deathbed chooses him to carry a final, vital message. He leaves at top speed, but meets obstacle after obstacle before even making it out of the palace. If he does get out, there will be thousands more. Or it is like K., the surveyor in *The Castle,* the expert of distances and specialist of locked doors: he begins his journey early, the Castle isn't far, but the road he follows leads nowhere. It is not that his path takes him away from the Castle but that he doesn't seem able to get closer to it before night begins to fall.

Kafka's letters also begin by subduing distance, but distance soon gets the upper hand and turns hostile. Rebuffed, it expands, multiplies, becomes infinitely divisible—Zenonian, as Daniel Oster calls it[1]—leaving Kafka and Felice now utterly separate: "I have the feeling of being outside a locked door behind which you live, and which will never be opened. Knocking is the only way of communicating" (March 3–4, 1913). In the epistolary love affair, there will always be a locked door, a doorway you have to pass through in order to truly meet the other, without detours or distractions; in order to find another person in whose presence you can *not* write, with whom you can be silent, with whom you can even sleep—who will put an end to those long nights fractured by insomnia and the composition of letters. The locked door will exist as long as letters exist. One might even say that there are no letters unless there are locked doors: "Well dearest, the doors are shut, all is quiet, I am with you once more" (December 15–16, 1912).

Lovers entrust their love to letters. Letters perform immediately, but immediacy by definition cannot last. Letters are pure mediation and themselves quickly become the principal obstacle to the immediacy they try to achieve. They should establish an unfailing continuity, they should ensure the constant and enchanting presence of the other, but instead they become a breeding ground for division, dissonance, and misunderstanding. The words that should prevent all forms of interruption become cracks and chinks that must be filled with other, ever stronger words. This explains the necessity of a linguistic passage from the formal to the informal, but it also explains the failure of such a passage:

> Dearest one! Can I really be sure of you now? The *Sie* glides as though on skates, it may have disappeared in the crack between two letters, one has to chase after it with letters and thoughts morning, noon, and night; but the *Du* stands firm; it stays here like your letter that doesn't move when I kiss it over and over again. But what a word that is! Nothing unites two people so completely, especially if, like you and me, all they have is words. *(November 14, 1912)*

"Du" is constant, it can be touched, held to the lips. Unlike the slippery "Sie," it wards off the danger of interruption—at least for a day or two, until its seemingly binding effect has seeped away. Felice's next letter is once again slow to arrive: "Look, the *'Du'* is nothing like the help I thought it would be. And today, only the second day, it isn't proving of much use" (November 15, 1912).

Interruption threatens constantly. Words plow through the distance between them, but they lose their meaning, their blood, before arriving at their destination. "Written kisses never arrive at their destination; the ghosts drink them up along the way. It is this ample nourishment which enables them to multiply so enormously" (March 1922), Kafka later wrote to Milena Jesenská. The letter writer wages an endless war against misunderstanding, interception, delay, and distance. Continuity and intimacy exist only in thought and imagination, in Kafka's dream of an endless letter from Felice:

> A mailman brought two registered letters from you, that is, he delivered them to me, one in each hand, his arms moving in perfect precision, like the jerking of piston rods in a steam engine. God, they were magic letters! I kept pulling out page after page, but the envelopes never emptied. I was standing halfway up a flight of stairs and (don't hold it against me) had to throw the pages I had read all over the stairs, in order to take more letters out of the envelopes. The whole staircase was littered

from top to bottom with the loosely heaped pages I had read, the resilient paper creating a great rustling sound. That was a real wish-dream! *(November 17, 1912)*

A real *Wunschtraum,* Kafka's image of endless debauchery—letters produced at will—inspired another dream (December 6–7, 1912) of a strange mechanism, a kind of telegram or fax machine which, when its button was pressed, would instantly spit out a letter from Berlin. (Kafka, of course, hated the telephone.) Another vision, almost his first daydream about Felice, set him permanently in front of the door to her house:

> If I were the Immanuelkirchstrasse mailman delivering this letter to your house, I wouldn't allow myself to be detained by any astonished member of your family, but would walk straight through all the rooms to yours and put the letter in your hands; or, better still, I would stand outside your door and keep on ringing the bell for my pleasure, a pleasure that would relieve all tension! *(October 13, 1912)*

The ultimate pleasure: to ring her doorbell forever outside the door, to meet her only on paper. The letter writer may dream of becoming his own mailman; he may blame the postal service for the interruptions and interceptions that occur and accuse it of keeping his letters from him. Kafka does not deprive himself of this pleasure: the postal service is his nemesis, his favorite symbol of deception, the mailman a diabolical Other, master of space and time who delays or steals the letters he is supposed to deliver. But at heart Kafka knows all too well that the distance appears not en route, but at the minute he writes the first words of a letter. And this is doubtless his true goal. His first letter to Felice is already somewhat diabolical and surprisingly precise in its demands. He is writing, he explains, in reference to a trip to Palestine they had agreed to take together during their meeting at the Brods' house:

> Now, if you still wish to undertake this journey—you said at the time you are not fickle, and I saw no signs of it in you—then it will be not

only right but absolutely essential for us to start discussing this journey at once. For we shall have to make use of every minute of our holiday, which in any case is far too short, especially for a trip to Palestine, and this we can do only by preparing ourselves as thoroughly as possible and by agreeing on all preparations. *(September 20, 1912)*

Kafka's request is ambiguous from the beginning: we should write to each other to prepare ourselves for a trip that, in all likelihood, we won't have time to take. Why not say, we should write to each other for no reason—or, more accurately, our correspondence should become an end in itself. The rest of the first letter leaves no doubt on this subject: "And yet, and yet . . . if doubts were raised, practical doubts I mean, about choosing me as a traveling companion, guide, encumbrance, tyrant, or whatever else I might turn into, there shouldn't be any prior objections to me as a correspondent—and for the time being this is the only thing at issue—and as such, you might well give me a trial."

Thus it all begins with a change in plans: the journey to Palestine becomes an epistolary voyage. In those years of budding Zionism, Palestine symbolized a new alliance and a new "human intercourse," as Kafka describes it. It represented a kind of exchange in which, as he repeatedly explains to Felice, he is irremediably incapable of participating. Palestine acquires a symbolic value in their relationship: it is the name given to the desire for union, a union that ultimately will be realized only through letters. Already in Kafka's first letter, the idea of "human intercourse" begins to blend into an epistolary trade. The existence of their correspondence itself precludes the possibility of the proximity it continues to promise. Palestine, the place, disappears into the distance and, retrospectively, Kafka's first sentences seem terribly ironic, since it is precisely in this emptiness, the epistolary space, that he will become a kind of guide for Felice, a teacher (assigning his future fiancée a veritable curriculum of letter writing)—but also an encumbrance and a tyrant.

* * *

For Kafka the letter writer, Palestine is out of reach and he will never have time to go there. With each letter, his vision of an alliance, of any common space and time, becomes slightly more blurred. Letters remove him from physical places, making space unshareable. Kafka sometimes claims that distance is his enemy. But the reader of his letters soon suspects that he has chosen this particular means of communication with Felice precisely in order to maintain or even produce distance. Distance is the sine qua non of their relationship: "Don't deceive yourself, dearest; the cause of the trouble lies not in the distance; on the contrary, it is this very distance that gives me at least the semblance of having some right to you, and I am holding on to that, insofar as one can hold on to uncertainties with uncertain hands" (March 9–10, 1913).

His bond with Felice frees him from the burdens of time and space. Kafka needs this correspondence because it creates a kind of private mental space that is his alone. Without letters, he would be left terrifyingly face to face with himself. But if the relationship with Felice were to extend beyond letters, if they were to go to Palestine together or to marry (which amounts to much the same thing), the distance would disappear again, would be transformed into a limited space. Felice, in Berlin, gives substance to the distance and to its defining quality: the impossibility of sharing. Felice defines a space simply by her exclusion from it and becomes the necessary witness to a Kafkaesque isolation:

> I have often thought that the best mode of life for me would be to sit in the innermost room of a spacious locked cellar with my writing things and a lamp. Food would be brought and always put down far away from my room, outside the cellar's outermost door. The walk to my food, in my dressing gown, through the vaulted cellars, would be my only exercise. I would then return to my table, eat slowly and with deliberation, then start writing again at once. And how I would write! From what depths I would drag it up! Without effort! For extreme concentration knows no effort. The trouble is that I might not be able to keep it up for

long, and at the first failure—which perhaps even in these circumstances could not be avoided—would be bound to end in a grandiose fit of madness. *What do you think, dearest? Don't be reticent with your cellar-dweller. (January 14–15, 1913)*

"Don't be reticent with your cellar-dweller" don't hide from his threatening madness, his radically unshareable singularity—a Kafka-esque marriage proposal, made without the possibility of fulfillment. "For who am I . . .? A shadow who loves you infinitely, but who cannot be drawn into the light" (January 5–6, 1913). The cellar-dweller needs a light outside his cave to contrast with the darkness inside. He needs a presence to vouch for his absence. Letters allow Kafka to show himself for the shadow that he is, forever on the threshold of light and dark. Exposed to the light, he would disappear or metamorphose into something monstrous, repulsive, purely ugly. (He insists that he is ugly.) Seen in the light, he would perhaps turn into Gregor Samsa, the hideous thing without name, unpresentable and terrifying to his loved ones, condemned to exile in his own home, done in by a rotten apple.

Incidentally, when illustrations were proposed for *The Metamorphosis,* Kafka demanded that there be no depiction of Gregor Samsa: "The insect itself cannot be depicted. It cannot even be shown from a distance . . . If I were to offer suggestions for an illustration, I would choose such scenes as the following: the parents and the head clerk in front of the locked door, or even better, the parents and the sister in the lighted room, with the door open upon the adjoining room that lies in darkness" (to Kurt Wolff, October 25, 1915). We can almost read *The Metamorphosis* as an allegory of what would happen if the letter writer were to step out of the shadows and expose his real self to another. The plot of *The Metamorphosis* was developed during the first weeks of Kafka's correspondence with Felice. It serves as a worrying footnote to the letters, suggesting what could happen after the correspondence ends. This is perhaps why Kafka looks forward to the "pleasure" of reading it aloud to Felice. He imagines holding her hand to ward off the fear that he plans to inspire: "I want to read it to you. Yes, that would be lovely, to read this story to you, while I would have to hold your hand, for the story is a little frightening. It is called *Metamorphosis,* and it would thoroughly scare you, you might not want to hear a word of it, for alas! I scare you enough every day with my letters" (November 23, 1912). The cockroach symbolizes the demise of the letter writer; it is a fragment of monstrous reality, a warning of what would happen if the epistolary distance were to disappear. If Kafka were ever to hold Felice's hand, he would immediately use his other hand to pull a copy of *The Metamorphosis* out of his pocket. He would turn himself into a cockroach, carefully closing the door that had opened between them, reintroducing distance and fear. His story issues from the same source as his letters, from the same heart, the same inhospitable space: "on the whole I am not too dissatisfied; but it is infinitely repulsive, and these things, you see, spring from the same heart in which you dwell and which you tolerate as a dwelling place" (November 24, 1912).

Nothing is more unbearable for the letter writer than the presence of the other. The other must always be absent, never taking on substance or form or sex. "Aside from other doubts, last time I was hampered by an actual fear of the reality of this girl behind the letters," he writes to Brod, a propos of a stay in Marienbad which will be the only moment of real "harmony" between Kafka and Felice, in July 1916. Kafka, in turn, makes himself invisible, a figure of darkness, and restricts his movements, trips, and meetings to writing. Months pass before Kafka and Felice can meet again in Berlin. In the meantime, hundreds of letters are written (half of the correspondence, which ends definitively in 1917). The second meeting is extremely brief, probably painful, and goes largely unmentioned in subsequent letters. It is simply an interruption in the correspondence and breaks a rhythm that will never be quite the same. Kafka and Felice's first rendezvous (not to be confused with their first, unforeseen meeting) deals a death blow to their epistolary relationship. It is the beginning of the end, a protracted ending drawn out over years—with two detours through engagement in 1914 and 1917. The last letter before Berlin, March 21, 1913: "Well, Felice, for the time being the letter writers take leave of each other, and the two who saw each other 6 months ago will be seeing each other again. Put up with the actual man as you have with the letter writer, no more! (This is the advice of one who loves you very much)." And in postscript: "Now that I have written this, it seems like an ugly fraud, but the presentation of the real man is about to begin."

Berlin, last stop. The letter writers take leave of one another, and the real man steps into the light. He does it in order to show that he is unpresentable, abject, that no relationship with him is possible. He has done everything in his power to avoid this moment. Having hidden for months behind his letters as if in "The Burrow" where nothing is ever supposed to happen, the cockroach finally comes out of his hole, as the rat will later (during the "idyll" in Marienbad): "It really seemed that the rat had been driven to its very last hole," he writes to Brod (mid-July 1916).

(Animal encounters: other rats and mice appear later in Kafka's world. After the final break with Felice, Kafka moves to a farm with his sister Ottla: "I live with Ottla in a good minor marriage" (to Brod, mid-September 1917). Life in Zürau would be wholly bucolic (no one to see, nothing to do but tend to his tuberculosis as tenderly as one cares for a plant) if it were not for the mice and rats, which race through his room every night. This is why, having played the rat, having imagined his home as a burrow or hole, he will unavoidably end up one day as one of the mouse folk so dear to Josephine.)

Prague to Berlin, just eight hours by train, barely enough time to write two long, voluptuous letters, and much less time than he spends waiting for answers and cursing mailmen: "Had I strung together the hours spent in writing to you and used them for a trip to Berlin, I should have been with you long ago, and could be looking into your eyes. And here I am, writing pages of absurdities as though life went on forever and ever and not a moment less" (December 4–5, 1912). Kafka takes his time—he has an eternity before him. Never during the course of these first six months does he jump on the train to Berlin, which carries only his letters. If he travels, it is out of professional obligation, with only a photo of Felice to accompany him. And sometimes with the sophist's consolation that his journey is taking him closer to Berlin—provided of course that it never takes him all the way there. For Kafka, real closeness can exist only in Prague, where the letters are waiting for him, all the more precious because he has been away. Moving closer to Berlin always distances him from Felice: "The only good thing about tomorrow's journey, for which I still have to prepare myself properly, is that I shall be several train-hours nearer to you. And then, if all goes well, I shall be back in Prague tomorrow afternoon, and race from the station to our porter. Letters, letters from you!" (December 7[8], 1912).

For five years Kafka is suspended, immobile, at a distance from everything, from Prague as from Berlin, from Felice as from himself, in a space where no meeting is possible. There will be other meetings, but they are always blocked by other doors. For example, July 3, 1916, during the stay in Marienbad, he notes in his *Diary:* "First day in Marienbad with F. Door to door, keys on either side." This trip, however, will be the only intimate moment between Felice and Kafka, who renew their relationship and decide wisely to write as little as possible, as if to avoid reopening the distance between them. Instead of writing, she occupies herself in Berlin with a home for Jewish refugee children, an activity that Kafka feels brings them closer (September 16, 1916). They are reunited for one last year, by children who are not their own, as they wait for the final break, which comes for Kafka in the form of tuberculosis, this time real. The collapse is now definitive: "For secretly I don't believe this illness to be tuberculosis, at least not primarily tuberculosis, but rather a sign of my general bankruptcy. I had thought the war could last longer, but it can't. The blood issues not from the lung, but from a decisive stab delivered by one of the combatants" (September 30, 1917). The shadow has won the battle: Marienbad was last year, and there will never be a voyage to Palestine.

For five years Kafka has given himself over to letters. He has lived outside himself, until called back to his body by tuberculosis or, rather, until tuberculosis finally makes his body unpresentable, forcing itself between him and Felice: "It was the sickness speaking, rather than myself, because I asked it to" (to Brod, late September 1917). He is definitely not back where he started, not only because he will never fully return to his body—which will spend the rest of its time traveling from sanatorium to sanatorium—but because he has, over these years, experienced distance; he has discovered space and its impossible dimensions. He has devoted himself to this space, produced by the writing of letters, and it in turn has produced literature. Kafka's first major works of fiction ("The Judgment," *The Metamorphosis,* certain chapters of *Amerika,* then *The Trial,* written after the first break with Felice) are all produced during his correspondence with Felice, and I have never been able to see the simultaneous emergence of the letters and the fiction as a simple coincidence. One point must be emphasized: for Kafka, the passage from reality to fiction required an extremely cruel gesture—the summoning and the dismissal of another—as if, in order to create fiction, a space had to be opened, another person had to be put at a distance. Felice always stays just out of Kafka's reach, but in the unique space between them—to which only he has access—lies his opening into literature.

After Felice, Kafka will have other liaisons, other openings and letters, most notably the devastating correspondence with Milena Jesenská, his Czech translator:

> Sometimes I feel we have a room with two doors on opposite sides and each of us is holding his doorknob and, at the bat of one person's eyelash, the other jumps behind his door, and now if the first person utters a single word, the second is sure to close the door behind him, so that

he can no longer be seen. He is bound to reopen the door, though, since it may be a room impossible to leave. If only the first person weren't exactly like the second, then he would be calm and pretend not to care in the slightest about the second; he would slowly go about ordering this room the way he would any other. But instead, he repeats the same thing at his door; occasionally even both people are standing behind their doors at the same time and the beautiful room is empty. *(June 3, 1920)*

Kafka and Milena: another story based on letters, where each of them is standing behind their doors in Prague and Vienna, with Gmünd in the middle, an impossible meeting point, an image of the beautiful empty room. Gmünd, echoing "mouth" in German *(mund)*, is a tongue twister, the unpronounceable opening that opens onto nothing. After the war it becomes a frontier town—balanced between two languages, pulsing with hostile customs officials, where everyone needs a visa (which takes them nowhere), where the only rendezvous that take place are illusory meetings between beings who may not even exist and who are tied together by the fear they inspire in each other.

"The reason I ask if you won't be afraid is because the person you write about does not exist and never did exist; the one in Vienna did not exist nor did the one in Gmünd, but if anyone did, it was the latter and may he be cursed" (September 1920), Kafka writes to Milena, after a meeting in Gmünd and in order to arrange one in Vienna. Gmünd is a place of transit, where nothing real takes place. It stands for missed meetings, impossible unions, and for Kafka's correspondence as a whole. Before Milena—whom he never really meets there—Kafka had tried to meet Grete Bloch, a friend of Felice's and the ambiguous (perhaps enamored) intermediary between the fiancés during their first entanglement; he later tries, not without some success, to involve Grete in an epistolary relationship. In Kafka's geography, in any case, Gmünd is the farthest place on earth from Palestine.

Variations on Immobility

From Kafka we turn to Gustave Flaubert and his letters to Louise Colet, another mechanism for producing distance and lost objects. For Flaubert (one of the writers who most fascinated Kafka[2]), meeting Louise Colet and becoming her lover was like taking holy orders, joining the cult of separation. In Louise's arms for the first time, in Paris, he becomes the hermit of Croisset. He feels closest to her at the moment he is saying goodbye, as if his thoughts can join hers only at a distance: "No sooner had I left you—and increasingly as I was borne further and further away—than my thoughts flew back toward you, more swiftly even than the smoke I saw billowing back from the train" (August 4–5, 1846). Their first night is barely over and already it is beginning to dissipate. He hurls himself onto the train, returns to Croisset, and begins one of the most famous series of letters in French literature. "I love you more than I loved you in Paris," he writes three days later. Is this why he will henceforth go to Paris as little as possible? He declares his love from the depths of the provinces, sends her frozen kisses, victims, as Kafka would say, of the ghosts who drink them up en route. "What have I done to make you cry still? When I am beside you I can wipe your tears away with a kiss, but at 30 leagues, the kiss I send you freezes in the air and you don't notice it on my letters when it arrives" (October 13, 1846). He loves Louise but prefers to lie low in Croisset, under pretext of supporting his mother through her double loss (both his father and his sister Caroline have recently died).

He must deal with his mother's grief but also with his own. We will see later that the immobility he requires is perhaps essentially a means of holding himself to his own mourning. He buries himself to keep the soul of his lost sister alive, and his letters to Louise ensure that his grief will last, that his own burial will be somehow substantial. The letters to Louise serve as a kind of reenactment of the loss of the loved object—a strange version of the Freudian bobbin. They are incredibly mournful, especially during the first months of the liaison. A goodbye that never ends (an echo to the mourning he cannot complete), they fixate on those remembered, celebrated moments of leavetaking: "I was the last to leave. Did you see how I was watching you until the very end? You turned around and walked away, and you disappeared from sight" (September 10, 1846). Seven years later, long after their first break, Flaubert still prefers to see Louise from behind, as if she is disappearing from sight; he still tries to be the one who leaves last, watching her train disappear in a cloud of steam: "When you disappeared, I went to stand on the bridge to watch the train pass by. That was all I saw. You were inside it; I watched it as long as I could and I listened as it went. The sky by Rouen was red with big, uneven purple stripes across it" (May 17, 1853).

Flaubert buries himself in the country, but on the condition that Louise stay constantly aware of it. He repeatedly reminds her that he is writing from another place, a place that serves him as a fundamentally welcome retreat from the world:

> Can I leave everything here and live in Paris? Impossible. If I were entirely free I would, for with you in Paris I wouldn't have the strength to go into exile—a project of my youth, which I shall carry out some day. For I want to live in a place where no one loves me or knows me, where the sound of my name causes only indifference, where my death or my absence costs no one a tear. *(August 9, 1846)*

If it were not for his mother, Flaubert would definitely go to Paris. But if Louise Colet did not exist to acknowledge his distance from the world, he would have to exile himself somewhere wholly out of reach. So his mother's mourning is not altogether useless. It guarantees the existence of distance between Flaubert and Louise, makes it as indestructible as an unconscious desire. He dreams of a no-man's-land between Croisset and Paris where he can escape from everything, from the tears, looks, and demands of others, even from his own name. In this space lies Mantes-la-Jolie, an unlikely locale for fleeting encounters. Flaubert and Louise meet there occasionally for a few quick embraces, poisoned in advance by their necessary brevity (Mantes-la-Jolie is Flaubert's Gmünd). The distance between Croisset and Paris is infinite because, in spite of his justifications, it is measured by Flaubert's desire to play dead: "I have dug my own hole and I live in it, taking care that the temperature stays always the same" (August 26, 1846).

The letters to Louise are a long series of variations on the theme of immobility—as if the purpose of love were to change nothing. Love without emotion: the art of not moving, of marinating, of closing oneself up like an oyster. At any rate, that is how Flaubert describes himself to his friend Ernest Chevalier, a week after meeting Louise: "I am the same as when you knew me, sedentary and calm in my narrow life, backside firmly planted in my armchair and pipe in my mouth. I work, I read, I do a little Greek, I ponder Virgil or Horace, I sprawl across a green leather couch I recently had made. Destined to marinate in one place, I've decorated my shell as I choose and live in it like a dreamy oyster" (August 12, 1846).

Flaubert's letters monopolize his emotions and movements. They flow one after the other, long and numerous; their author does not follow them. It takes the first breakup with Louise in 1848 to make him move. Without letters to assure him of the distance between him and the world, he resorts to real distance and in 1849, despite his mother's continuing grief, the hermit of Croisset sets off for Egypt. There in the Orient, his accomplishment in apathy is astonishing. He cultivates the science of immobility. He travels in order to dig himself deeper into his hole, to create a void within and around himself. So he comes closer, perhaps, to the mental space he needs to write in earnest: not *La tentation de Saint Antoine* (which, in its first version, he considered a failure) but *Madame Bovary*. In the shadow of the pyramids, he begins to imagine the countryside of Normandy.

In June 1851 Flaubert returns to Croisset. In July he is reunited with Louise; the correspondence starts up again. On September 20 he begins *Madame Bovary*. An epistolary distance replaces the true separation he experimented with in Egypt. Like Felice, Louise is summoned in order to be dismissed, excluded from a space that is now explicitly that of literature, and exists only as long as she is forbidden to enter it. "My work is beginning to progress again. I've finally recovered from the disturbance of my little trip to Paris.—My life is so still that a grain of sand disturbs it. I need absolute immobility to be able to write. I think best when lying on my back with my eyes closed. The least noise repeats itself in me in a prolonged echo which takes forever to die" (April 15, 1852).

Flaubert repeatedly begs Louise not to disturb him, to make no noise, to be a silent entity, a voice filtered and muffled by letters. He keeps his visits to Paris as brief as possible. He asks her to wait. The new contract between them is apparently clear: as soon as he finishes his novel, he will move to Paris and read *Bovary* aloud to her, this book that for the moment he keeps completely to himself.[3]

> Do you know what I am waiting for? The moment, the hour, the minute, when I will write the last line of some long work of mine, like *Bovary* or others, and, gathering together all the pages, I will bring them to you, read them to you in that special voice with which I soothe myself, and you will listen to me, I will see you soften, tremble, and open your eyes. That will be my absolute joy.—You know that I will have to find lodging in Paris at the beginning of next winter.—We will inaugurate it, if you like, with the reading of *Bovary*. It will be a celebration. *(June 19, 1852)*

Next winter, then the winter after that: Flaubert repeatedly postpones the celebration with Louise, postpones the moment of pleasure when she will tremble at the sound of his voice—which for the time being soothes only himself. His letters are now filled with promises, but the reasons to delay their fulfillment multiply and Flaubert is forced, time after time, to put off his arrival. Thus, to our great benefit, he creates one of the most important poetics and literary ethics of recent history.

The letters to Louise are based on an impossible promise. Their fundamental premise is that distance will win out, that Louise will always be the absent one, caressed by a voice she cannot hear, a voice that speaks hopelessly to no one in the night in Croisset, a voice that perhaps must be lost to someone else before it can make itself heard in writing. (He shouts in Croisset and is heard in letters in Paris: style is a woman he does not address, or whom he addresses less and less.) It is common practice to write to warn someone before you arrive. But when, in order to write, you must first lose the other person, the chances that you will ever actually arrive are slim. Flaubert finishes *Madame Bovary* in 1856. His visits to Paris become more frequent, but he no longer sees Louise (they broke the relationship off, finally, in 1854). It is as if, once the book is launched, Louise's presence, or more precisely her absence, is no longer necessary. "I must decrease so that Madame Bovary may increase," Louise might have told herself had she read *Hérodias* (which, unfortunately, hadn't yet been published). Flaubert's letters to Louise depict an absence, a solitude, day after day of separation, a prospect always on the horizon. What of Louise Colet after 1854? She is not entirely hidden in the grass, but almost. She has become so much a part of his writing, through letters, that she is a shadow in his words. She is their destination.

Postscript: March 6, 1855, a letter from Flaubert to Louise, both in Paris, written a year after their separation: "I was told that you took the trouble to come here to see me three times last evening. I was not in. And, fearing lest persistence expose you to humiliation, I am bound by the rules of politeness to warn you that *I shall never be in*" (March 6, 1855). When he chooses, Flaubert can cut things off without the least ambiguity.

The Unpredictable

We are all familiar with his cork-lined room, his attacks of asthma, and his increasingly methodical reclusion in his room on the boulevard Haussmann from which he refuses all visits and invitations, other than a few rare friends received in bed between fumigations. We also know how he goes out unexpectedly, wearing a fur coat in midsummer, and arrives late to receptions, just as the last plates are being cleared from the tables.

Marcel Proust reaches a full understanding with distance. Some place it on the European scale, between Prague, Berlin, and Vienna. Others position it between the capital and the provinces. Proust moves it to Paris, within Paris, underneath his own roof. He picks up where Kafka leaves off, with a sickness that condemns him to an unshareable space, an air that is literally unbreathable for others: "I do hope to be able to come. As for the opposite (your visit here), that is much more difficult. My room is almost always full of a thick steam which would be as intolerable for your breathing as it is necessary for mine" (to Madame Caillavet, April 20, 1915). He lives on another planet, breathes in another atmosphere, which prevents him from receiving visitors and makes it impossible for others to receive him: "Many thanks for Nice, but, alas, I have long since ceased to be 'invitable.' My constant fumigations don't allow me to stay with friends, or, at least, they make it so inconvenient for them that it becomes, instead, a torture for me. Two years ago, the Clermont-Tonnerres 'neutralized' a whole section of Glisolles so that I could be 'at home' there and I couldn't make myself go" (to Madame Catusse, February 1915).

Proust places himself in quarantine (to use Alain Buisine's expression).[4] As it grows less and less inhabitable and less and less presentable, his body becomes a barrier that the years will render almost insurmountable. The more it abandons him, the more it cuts him off from society. He speaks constantly of his weight loss, writing every word as if it were his last: "Forgive me for ending my letter a little abruptly—letter writing is forbidden to me because of the enormous amount of weight I have lost and it has taken a great effort to write to you" (to Madame Hugo Finaly, November 24, 1913). His body becomes an unpresentable, elusive third party preventing all form of

meeting between Proust and the rest of the world. It is as unpredictable and evil as the postal service was for Kafka. Bound to this body
are the letters that disperse its news: "Bedridden and unable to write,
I want you to know, however, that I don't stop thinking of you, with
all of my hopeless heart" (to Francis de Croisset, January 6, 1906).
"The state of my health unfortunately prevents me from telling you
at length (in fact I'm absolutely forbidden even to write) that your
letter filled me with gratitude—and astonishment" (to André Maurel,
January 1906).

For over twenty years Proust writes several thousand letters about
his illness. He is the author of the longest medical bulletin in the history of French literature. His letters exist primarily to symbolize the
distance from the world his body has condemned him to—and they
have the advantage of doubling this distance. One would be wrong
to see these letters as a form of compensation for his isolation, the
only means of communication possible for an invalid: Proust tells little
about himself in his letters (he almost never mentions his writing) and
demands little news of others. Communication is not his forte. His
letters are often purely formal. He writes in order to say that his body
will barely allow him to write, as if he already had one foot in the
grave. He speaks of his illness and his illness speaks through him; it
becomes a form of literature.

No one will ever really know which came first, the sickness or the
epistolary urge: the facts are lost in an adolescent fog. But it is clear
that the two develop in parallel, like the two fronts of a military maneuver to distance others. The illness becomes a stamp of authenticity
that makes the distance marked by letters irrefutable.

For Proust, Gmünd (the impossible rendezvous) is located in the six-
teenth arrondissement. There, without leaving his home, he organizes
his separation from those close to him—including his mother, with
whom he manages to live for several years communicating almost exclusively through notes, getting up when she goes to bed and vice

versa, leaving his messages in the soup tureen in the dining room where their meals are no longer taken together. He begins to make use of his asthma attacks to exempt himself from the usual rhythms of life. Restricted spatially, he manages to distance himself from others with time and routine. A few hours, or even less, can constitute as much distance as a thousand miles. One of the wonders of time: you can avoid the other, all others, without moving.[5]

What Kafka concentrates in the distant Felice, Proust disseminates throughout Paris. He does not limit himself to one exchange of letters; his correspondence survives through the proliferation of its participants, with whom he makes a thousand different impossible arrangements. What he shares with his correspondents are missed meetings, the time he can never find to see them. Asthma always intervenes—not only the attacks in progress, but the ones he can feel coming on that make all arrangements tentative, often causing him to cancel in advance: "Even if today's outing doesn't provoke a major attack tomorrow, I will only know towards four o'clock whether I will be able to go to Bing's at six, and that is probably too late to let you know, and also very uncertain and unlikely, and not very sensible, even if I am not in too much pain" (to Marie Nordlinger, January 30, 1904).

He writes numerous letters not only to cancel plans already made but also to explain why he cannot make plans, to replace tentative arrangements with the announcement of oncoming attacks: "I have some important things to tell you. Unfortunately as I went out this evening (indeed that's the reason why I have these important things to tell you), tomorrow Wednesday (today by the time you receive this note) I shall have a bad attack and be unable to see anyone. Will you, however, just in case, telephone me around half past nine in the evening" (to Emmanuel Bibesco, June 11–12, 1907). Proust's correspondence is based on a defiance of time, a failure of its common measure. He looks for time that the other has lost, for time that only he can claim. He writes in order to make his time unshareable, to transform it into a mental space that, through the exclusion of his correspondents, is guaranteed to be his alone.

His motif is not, like that of Flaubert or Kafka, the obviously impossible rendezvous, but the unpredictable one: a meeting planned and then called into question or, inversely, one that is unlikely and then fixed at the last moment, often too late. His letters plot out such unpredictable meetings that they end up substituting for them, as this letter to Bernard Grasset, among many others, testifies:

> I have written you a very long letter because in my current state of health and living in a constant fumigation, I cannot receive visitors, and it is difficult for me to visit others because if, by chance, I am feeling better one evening, I take advantage of it, I get up and go out, but, unfortunately, without having any advance warning of these rare remissions. If, however, you tell me that you are always at home on a certain day, or at certain times, if luck had it that I happened to feel better, I would call to ask if you could see me. But as this is all very unlikely, I will put you in contact with one of my friends who will be able to see you for me when you wish. *(February 24, 1913)*

Proust's life is played out in a giant casino: his relationships, meetings, outings, movements, all a game of roulette. Luck and chance decide things for him, no prior agreement is ever possible. He will only come and see you if he can do it unexpectedly: "For more than fifteen years, the only journeys I've been able to take (if you can call a few hours of travel a journey) have been made on condition that they could be decided only an hour in advance" (to Louis de Robert, January 30, 1913). He writes to warn you that if he arrives it will be without warning. Or he warns you too late, fait accompli, a sudden departure for Cabourg and a just as sudden return:

> I was very sad to have left Cabourg without having seen you . . . But my departure wasn't at all planned. I went out, heading for Houlgate, and having decided to stay on for several more days. But, on the way to Houlgate, I was suddenly so strongly taken by the desire to be in Paris

that, to avoid indecision, I decided to leave immediately, without my things or any luggage . . . I have been so ill since my arrival that I don't know if I'll come back; in truth I doubt it. *(to Charles d'Alton, August 1913)*

He systematically leaves without a forwarding address and only sends it when he has already moved on. Or he writes to warn his correspondents that no one must know of his return or his new address: "No one (because of the unbelievable state in which I've arrived and remained, fever, asthma, etc.) must know that I am here" (to Madame Catusse, December 30, 1906). If no one must know, it might be wiser not to tell anyone. But then Proust does not write all these letters so that people will forget about him.

From unexpected departure to missed meeting, Proust makes himself so unpredictable as to disappear. His letters establish him in a singular point of space and time. They give him a place and a temporality free of all exterior influence. This space is first of all that of dream and desire and, second, that of writing. A man of withdrawal and shadow, Proust still never stops desiring the other, all others, never stops thinking of them—in fact, it is just about the only thing that seems to interest him: "If you haven't had a letter from me since my arrival here (August 8), it's not because I have spent ONE DAY without thinking of you, and with a thought that wasn't only a memory but a desire to see you, a desire to arrange things so that I could see you. And then . . . you know, you understand without me telling you. I haven't left the hotel once since my arrival" (to Madame Straus, August 22, 1912).

He will consider any movement, any travel, if it remains imaginary, pure thought and desire. Letters replace cars and trains. And when he does move, he goes nowhere, to dream more clearly of unseen friends: "I came to your house on the off chance, but much too late to warn you. It was twenty or quarter to eleven when I arrived at the triple arched door. Everything was dark, on every floor. I let the motor run a little to see if a curtain would open, and nothing having happened,

I didn't dare ring, thinking you had perhaps gone to bed" (to Madame de Caillavet, April 23, 1915). He goes suddenly and unexpectedly to a friend's house, but stops at the door. Immobile, in the dark, he leaves the motor running and dreams of the woman he will write to soon to let her know—with the exact time as proof—that they almost saw each other.

Proust: a life spent in letters, throwing off schedules, using unpredictability to escape a sense of time belonging to the other. In the beginning the *other* that Proust wishes to distance himself from is his mother. On reading their correspondence, one sees that nothing is less accurate than the image of faultless intimacy that Proust so frequently vaunted, especially after her death. In fact, her death was necessary to overcome the distance between them. Their intimacy during her life had a lethal undertone and their relationship was stifling. Letters, acting as intermediary, gave them some distance; they allowed Proust to plot out his own time and space.

This begins to be clear in his apparently trivial and informal letters, written during their first separations, consisting almost exclusively of health bulletins and detailed explanations of his schedule. Proust is twenty-five, his mother in Evian:

> To continue what I told you in my last letter, I finished dinner and went out at 10 P.M., came in again at 11:30, and was in bed by a quarter past twelve. Now comes a great blow. After a fumigation (alas, I'd already had to have one in the middle of dinner) I took neither amyl, nor valerian, nor anything else (except a *tisane* and bicarbonate) and I felt much better for it. I was woken up again far too early, but as I was sleepy from dining late . . . I dropped off again in a series of dozes or meditations like Papa's, for ten minutes at a time, until 9:30. *(September 16, 1896)*

As his many detailed accounts confirm, he feels that he owes his mother an explanation of his time, just as he owes her his life and body. Contrary to appearances, however, these letters represent a first separation. It is better to pass on the news of one's health and activities than to share them with another. The letters, by accounting for the physical aspects of his life, allow his soul to withdraw to an unreachable space.

Year after year, in letter after letter to his mother, Proust maps out the timetable of his waking and sleeping hours, his insomnia, his meals. He describes his attacks, coughs, indigestion, diarrhea, in unsparing detail. It is as if this is the penalty he must pay in order to escape. It is as if the body has this many symptoms and maladies only for him to hide behind, as if without them to report he would lose all possibility of intimacy: "I would rather have attacks and please you than displease you and not have any" (May 1903). His mother is happy only when something is wrong (especially in matters of health), and reciprocally he can only stand her when he is ill, with his quarantine and unusual hours to protect him.

Healthy, Proust has no way to loosen the hold that others have over him. And Madame Proust has always been the emblematic figure of this hold. (I am not discussing their real relationship here: after her death, even before, others substitute for her). Healthy, he is required to share and account for his time. As soon as he feels better, as soon as he tries to live like other people, to go out, to see friends, his mother begins—according to him—to poison his existence, scolding him for wasting time, for not organizing his life as she would like: "The truth is that as soon as I feel better, the life that makes me feel better exasperates you and you demolish everything until I feel ill again. This isn't the first time. I caught cold last night; if it turns to asthma, which it's sure to in the present state of affairs, I have no doubt that you'll be good to me again, when I'm in the same state as this time last year" (December 6, 1902).

Health signifies time that must be devoted, if not to his mother, to an occupation that she approves of: a regular job and not what she refers to as a "cocottes' dinner," which to Proust's chagrin she refuses to hold at the house (his space is never sufficiently his own). He cannot enjoy health—it is time that he cannot claim because it is confiscated by other people's desires. His efforts when healthy are never enough:

> I remember telling you, early in December, when you complained of my intellectual inactivity, that you were really too impossible, that confronted with my veritable resurrection, instead of admiring it and loving what had made it possible, you insisted on my starting to work at once. But I complied, and took up just the work you wished . . . I'm still more or less alive, and despite the enormous amount of work I've turned out, you keep telling me day after day how amazed and pleased So-and-so was to see me so well, and I did manage, crushing as it was for me, to attend Robert's wedding. All this isn't enough for you, or rather it's nothing to you, and you'll continue to disapprove of everything I do until I fall ill again as I did two years ago. Even that wretched *Renaissance latine*. You manage to poison the day it comes out for me. *(March 9, 1903)*

Until his relapse, when his state of health precludes all reproaches, his mother poisons his time. Or, perhaps more accurately, Proust uses her to symbolize whomever or whatever is poisoning his time and space. Distance and the epistolary relationship become necessary to ward off what he cannot bear in the presence of another. The relationship between Proust and his mother has been much discussed. If I emphasize it here, it is because the ambivalence of their relationship perfectly illustrates the Proustian epistolary ethic. The other is tolerable only as long as she does not threaten the space-time the subject needs in order to exist. She is tolerated only from a distance, and from a distance becomes absolutely necessary, even desirable, because she allows the subject to emerge and present himsef in the space he has found. Proust is never as close to his mother as when they are apart (when one of them is away on holiday), and similarly he is never as close to himself as when he is elsewhere, traveling.

August 11, 1904: Proust is between La Rochelle and Dinard on board the yacht *Hélène*, named after the symbol of all illegitimate desire. (Is this the yacht he later dreams of giving to Albertine, the model for the plane, never used, intended for Agostinelli?) He is taking a cruise, one of his last trips, one of the last occasions to get some air, "air that is very different from that of our dining room," he stresses to his mother. He has rarely felt so good. He writes his mother one of the longest letters we have: "I'm going to reply in minute detail to all the questions you might ask me." A detailed report follows: few asthma attacks, little trouble breathing, three meals a day (two more than usual), eaten at normal hours. He even decides to prolong the cruise. Getting away from it all seems to have done him some good. But writing, and creating the epistolary distance, also seems to do him some good, to such an extent that in the letter it seems to be the primary cause of his well-being: "Since writing to you I've warmed up and no longer have any asthma. As in an opera, you were bending over me as I wrote, and the soothing effect of our conversation removed the last traces of oppression. I think I shall leave tomorrow morning. But I shall have to start early. And having eaten scarcely anything at lunchtime I shall have to have some dinner and that will prevent me from going to bed early. Complicated!"

Writing letters has cured his asthma, but it does not mean that he is ready to come home. In order to see his mother, he would have to leave early in the morning and thus go to bed early. The cruise is not over yet and the problems of scheduling are beginning already, the shadows of predicted illness. Only writing letters can forestall the course of events. It provides him with a time of remission and convalescence, "the soothing effect of our conversation." Mother and son can be reunited at the bedside only from this distance: "It seems to me so odd, when I'm tucked away in your heart and have you perpetually within reach of my thoughts and my affection, when I speak to you in my imagination a hundred times a minute and hug you no less often, to think that my letter must go such a long way to find you and will reach you long after I've written it." Writing from the yacht, Proust manages for once to combine distance with absolute closeness.

Heimat

Few writers have left behind them so impressively voluminous a correspondence as Rainer Maria Rilke. And few have seemed so systematically concerned with finding a separate, unshareable space, inhabited only by the poetic urge. Many of Rilke's letters are not only the footnotes to his creative moments, but also the inspiration. As with Kafka and Proust, letters allow a space where poetic creation is possible.

He was born in Prague, like Kafka, but returned there very little during his adult life. He felt neither Czech nor Austrian, sometimes barely even Germanophone. Like most writers in the German language at the time, he spent the better part of his time traveling or living abroad—in Russia, Paris (where his decisive meeting with Rodin took place), Italy, Spain, Egypt. But for Rilke perhaps more than for others, this kind of movement became essential, a sort of ethos. He wanders through turn-of-the-century Europe in search of the perfect place to live and write—and finds it perhaps, just a few years before his death, in the small chateau in Muzot, Switzerland, near Sierre, an area that is, like Rilke, both French and German. In this area of synthesis he rediscovers even the qualities he admired in Spain and Egypt.

Rilke's life is broken up into a multitude of shorter and longer stays, as if he is perpetually paying visits or taking a vacation. He is in the grip of a kind of centrifugal force which, for years (at least until he settles in Muzot), pushes him to travel constantly. During this time it is less important for him to *see* something new than it is for him to *be* in a new place, an "elsewhere" that will generate an interior space. He tries on spaces like a new suit of clothes.[6] He stays nowhere long and is never where you thought he was. When you think he is in Paris, he replies from Bremen: "A few days ago, impatient with myself, I left Paris quite abruptly" (to the Princess Marie von Thurn und Taxis, July 13, 1910). He accepts an invitation to visit the same princess in Lautschin (in Bohemia), but returns to Paris without having gone to see her. Then one more trip to Leipzig, Berlin, Munich, and back to

Paris again. There he begins to dream of Toledo, where he cannot go until after an important trip to Duino, on the Adriatic, in one of the princess' other homes, and another stay in Venice. His biographies are divided up geographically into his Russian, Parisian, and Swiss chapters.

What is he running away from? His mother perhaps. He suggests this once, in a letter to Lou Andreas-Salomé (his former mistress and most regular confidante), almost too perfectly for the psychoanalyst she later becomes:

> When I have to see this lost, unreal woman who is connected with nothing, who cannot grow old, I feel how even as a child I struggled to get away from her, and fear deep within me lest after years and years of running and walking I am still not far enough from her, that somewhere inwardly I still make movements that are the other half of her embittered gestures, bits of memories that she carries about broken within her. *(April 15, 1904)*

If it were absolutely necessary to identify the origin of his centrifugal force, we could place it here. But Rilke's mother could easily be just a temporary incarnation of the force behind his constant movement.

So he perfects the art of never being where he is supposed to be (to the extent that he is no longer ever really expected to be anywhere); the art also of never being where he himself expects to be. He oscillates between being where he will be and where he used to be. He needs Europe—his aristocratic and romantic contacts there—in order to experience the division of the subject. Is he really writing about Leipzig? He has just left Lautschin, but he is still somehow there; he is already in Paris, but not quite there yet. Wherever he may be in reality, he is still traveling, one foot in the car that carries him and the other on the train he would have preferred to take:

> What am I doing, dear Princess, addressing this letter from "Leipzig," when in fact I will be arriving there only bit by bit, in a few days; for the moment, in my heart and mind, I have still too many reasons for being with you, on the way to Paris. I do not know when you will be arriving

there, but perhaps tomorrow; as you can guess, there are quite a few instants where I feel compelled to arrive there as soon as possible as well. On the other hand, I am still pretty much attached to Lautschin, and driving away from there in a car didn't leave me with a convincing feeling of having left; one truly departs only by train, everyone sees it, but like this—? And then, I am still very much in the mind-frame of the trip. *(to Marie von Thurn und Taxis, August 25, 1911)*

"In a few days": but he will be in Berlin by then. He wanders through countries, cities, in search of lost fragments of himself, as if he will meet himself somewhere and thus be able to establish or reestablish a continuity.

But this continuity consists only in the never-ending track of his movements. The only permanence he can hold on to is the one he creates through his letters. "If there is something I do need now, Princess, it is your letters, thanks to which everything progresses; what I am hoping for in the near future, as far as tranquility and security go, lies in your letters, and is more than just a promise, although as yet unrealized," he writes to the princess (September 23, 1911). "Your letters are for me like those very rare things, which consitute a continuity from what has been in the past to what will be in the future, and I am holding on to them as a crutch—if I only knew where they will lead me," he writes to her again several years later (September 6, 1915). Only letters make his solitude bearable, only letters give him continuity; hence the enormous volume and absolute necessity of his correspondence.

The space occupied by letters, however, is fragile and uncertain. Rilke's correspondence is pure transition, a passage from one non-place to another. "If I only knew where they will lead me": Rilke is always passing through, in transit, at a distance from everything. This is the foundation of his lifestyle and his relationship with others, as he describes them as early as 1903 (after separating from his wife Clara), in a letter to Lou Andreas-Salomé: "My habitat, what was it to me, other than a strange place for which I had to work, and what are the people close to me, other than visitors who do not want to leave. How much do I let myself go every time I wish to be of some service to them; how much do I distance myself from myself and yet remain unable to reach them, getting caught on the way from myself to them, and, as if on a journey, I no longer know where I am, nor how much of myself is with me, and within reach" (August 8, 1903). Caught on the road between himself and others, losing himself when close to others, finding himself again when he leaves them: his letters come to signify this paradoxical space. Thanks to his letter writing, Rilke is able to establish himself in distance; the continuity of his correspondence counterbalances the elements in him which will not "take," which require him to be perpetually in motion, traveling and visiting others.

In the mature works (after 1900 or so), alongside the cosmopolitan Rilke who is at home anywhere, there appears his opposite, his double, a Rilke obsessed with the creation of his own space. This space exists, for many years, only in letters, as Rilke waits for the poetic work that will give it a more satisfactory form. The completion of the *Elegies* seems to provide it: "I am my own contemporary again," he writes to Nanny Wunderly-Volkart (February 15, 1922) in a letter that is almost a victory bulletin. (The *Elegies* are actually a far more ephemeral victory than they first seem.) His work attempts to provide a *Heimat,* a means of meeting himself and becoming his own contemporary—a stay-at-home who needs no contact with others: "I know that I too may ask and seek for no other realizations than those of my work; only there is my home, there are the people who are truly close to me, the women I need, and the children who will grow up and live a long time" (to Lou Andreas-Salomé, August 8, 1903). From one house to the next, Rilke is a person for whom all social ties lead to a destruction of the self. He comments on this in the same letter (a beautiful letter concerned principally with Rodin's ability to inhabit an entirely unique space): "There are others who are fundamentally solitary, and they are not destined to be sociable; from the very relationship arises a threat and an enmity; the home they build weighs on them, because they lack a homeland to support it, and with the ones they love, things get so close that there is no chance for distance" (to Lou Andreas-Salomé, August 8, 1903). Several weeks later, again in a letter to Lou, he speaks of his inability to become *real*, to form a truly consistent subject:

> In the past I believed that everything would change as soon as I had a home, a wife, and a child, things of real and undeniable value; I believed that I would become more visible, tangible, and real myself. But look, even if Westerwede did indeed *exist* and was real—because I built the house and everything that it contained myself—it remained a reality *outside* of myself, into which I could not integrate myself, and with which I could not identify . . . It is only when I work (which is so rarely) that I become real and exist, that I occupy space like a thing. *(November 13, 1903)*

Rilke takes on form and substance only through writing. But, as he constantly complains, the days he spends working are rare, and become more so later. His creative work-space does not materialize. It evades him despite, or perhaps partly because of, the completion of certain texts (such as *The Notebooks of Malte Laurids Brigge*). And his provisional epistolary space remains necessary, a stepping stone on the way to something more complete. On this level, Rilke's correspondence is always a transitional medium, a passage from one thing to another, toward a work or a space that has yet to be formed. He considers his letters an integral part of his oeuvre, but generally qualifies them as a practice or preparation for his real work. His writing takes place on two levels, with the poetic on the higher plane and the epistolary *(zum verbriefen)* on the lower. His correspondence, which expands at a dizzying rate over his years of creative "sterility," becomes a solid form between the two blanks in his life: the first being the social duties and ties (especially marriage) he tries to avoid, and the second, the work itself. Letters provide a tangible replacement for the mental space that Rilke's abandoned work used to create. They give foreground to a life passed at a distance, or in the distance. They allow Rilke to give in to his inescapable urge for separation and give solidity and continuity to his otherwise uncertain existence.

The epistolary space becomes a second *Heimat,* a home rather than a homeland: there is something more maternal in the word *Heimat* than in "homeland," something more intimate, and for Rilke something more secret or *heimlich.* This becomes clear in a letter to Nanny Wunderly-Volkart, one of Rilke's mainstays during the last years of his life:

> God knows why I entertain so many relationships; sometimes I believe that it is a substitute for a homeland, as if with this vast net of influences I have been given, in spite of everything, the possibility of subtly being everywhere; it also often appears to me that I am doing it for someone else, for Ruth maybe? As if I were actually not perceiving her as my child, in the sense that I could tailor and prepare her world out of my own. *(January 14, 1920)*

Rilke finds a substitute homeland in his letters. And only in letters does he manage to become a father: not a guest in his own home, but a whole person presiding over a world he can pass on to his daughter (soon lost from sight after the failure of his marriage).

This obsession with *Heimat* explains one of the peculiarities of Rilke's letters: the enormous amount of space he devotes to mundane or friendly exchanges. Kafka and Flaubert use letters as a tool in their constant sacrifice of the object of desire. The recipient of these letters is required, against her will, to recognize Kafka or Flaubert as inhabiting a separate space from which she is excluded; the letters do not form a space or continuity but become instead a nonplace, a controlled rupture (this also applies to Proust, though in a slightly different way). Rilke, a great melancholy seducer and master of long-distance passion, also used this strategy effectively, as in his letters to "Merline" Klossowska. These letters are often a veritable hymn in praise of a shared separation, which is mutually accepted and considered imperative for the maintenance of the space that Rilke needs.[7]

In the body of letters as a whole, however, this type is relatively rare. Rilke masters the kind of separation necessary for the production of a great work. He sends kisses through the mail as others send pearls: "Oh, if only, by caressing the paper between my hands, I were able to transmit some of that infinite tenderness of which I have never been able to give you enough; I even wonder whether in fact you have had any, my hands having remained, Dearest, so inexhaustibly brimming" (to Merline, September 17, 1920). Too many kisses spoil the writing: none of Rilke's love letters express an involvement comparable to Kafka's or Flaubert's. Or they express it only occasionally, interspersed with other kinds of letters. His most charged and involved epistolary exchanges are, in fact, with a series of neutral and well-wishing confidantes, aristocratic (at least in spirit) patrons of the arts—a chain of guardian angels spread out across Europe: the Princess von Thurn und Taxis or Nanny Wunderly-Volkart or Lou Andreas-Salomé. Begun at very different points of his life, all three of these epistolary exchanges continue until his death in 1926.

Letters create a *Heimat* for Rilke, not by forbidding another to enter it but by establishing relationships devoid of desire. He undertakes, with these privileged correspondents, a voluminous exchange of letters in which the question of desire is never raised—voluminous perhaps in order to preclude the question, to avoid all possibility of a closer tie. What he gains is a set of correspondents who understand his need for solitude and who even take it upon themselves to ensure its fulfillment by buying him the secluded space he longs for. Settled in Berg, near Zurich, (thanks to Nanny), he writes to Marie von Thurn und Taxis to thank her for having approved of his plan: "That you had not yet approved of my project had so far been the only imperfection within the perfect world of Berg: now you have rectified that; a caterpillar, spinning myself gradually into my *cocoon*, I wrap myself up bit by bit in my growing beard" (December 15, 1920). The letters he writes to his patrons, as well as those he receives from them, become guarantees of the self-sufficiency and solitude he needs: they are the markers, not of desire but of its absence, the proof that he has nothing to answer for, nothing *unheimlich.* "I feel so much at home in your letters," Rilke writes to Lou (January 24, 1920), when trying to decide whether to risk a cure with the psychoanalyst Gebsattel. (He decides against it, apparently preferring to confide in the former mistress who knows him so well.) With his confidantes to watch over him, he will never have to answer for anything. Letters are for him a vast, complex undertaking to avoid what is alien, a means of preventing any kind of subjective expropriation that would destroy his feeling of being at home.

So he avoids writing too many love letters or exposing himself too fully to another person. The liaisons and passions he does experience leave him feeling dispossessed, he often complains: "But I *must* free my life from the influence to which it has been increasingly subjected. It is only here that I have felt to what degree my life, under the daily pressure of that other life, was losing its own form and, in a way, had begun to assume a different density" (to Nanny Wunderly, March 3, 1920). The "other life" he refers to here is that of a certain Angela Guttmann, but the scenario of dispossession is always the same; or at least it is presented in the same way to the uninvolved third party who helps him to establish his desire-free space, his solitary, intimate *Heimat.*

Kafka, Flaubert, and Proust write to create a void, to open up a unique space between themselves and their correspondents. Rilke, on the contrary, expects the other to provide him with his most private, personalized space. The lack of romantic involvement in his correspondence is thus absolutely imperative. With Marie von Thurn und Taxis or Nanny Wunderly, this requirement is fulfilled. Rilke finds his first refuge in Duino, in the princess' domain, and is able to begin the *Elegies* (and to complete the first version of at least two of them). In Duino he is able to withdraw from the world into his own almost secret space (the princess herself is elsewhere during his stay): "What a blessing that you are willing to hide me in Duino. I wish to stay there like a refugee, under a different name, and you will be the only one to know that it is me" (September 17, 1911). He begins writing the poems that will become the *Duino Elegies*. Finishing them eleven years later, he remembers Duino (although he never went back there—the chateau was bombed during the war and was more or less in ruins), and the *Elegies* are prefaced by a notation of their source rather than a dedication: "From the domain of the Princess von Thurn und Taxis-Hohenlohe." They are not addressed to the princess, but they belong to her as the patron who made their composition possible. "The entire work is *yours,* Princess, how could it be otherwise!" (February 11, 1922). Rilke spends only a few months at Duino, but it is enough for him to consider himself a native. A few weeks later, en route to Spain, he sends this note to the princess: "I am sending you my very best regards from Bayonne. I signed the hotel register, of course, as someone coming from Duino; I started there, it was my departure point and cannot be changed; now I will move on, travel, and develop" (October 30, 1912).

As a provider of space, Marie von Thurn und Taxis also becomes a guardian of Rilke's writing, as Nanny Wunderly did later. While the princess furnished Rilke with living space at Duino, Nanny brought him first to Berg, near Zurich, then to Muzot, where an important part of the poetic work was written. Nanny is not a muse but a housing agent par excellence (unlike Felice or Louise who are, in spite of themselves, the source of inspiration). She supervises everything, even the most mundane task, ensures that Rilke finds the furniture and the household objects he needs, organizes his finances, finds housekeepers for him, and so on, all through the mail. The hundreds of letters about household affairs that Rilke addresses to Nanny Wunderly can seem far removed from literature. Together, however, they make up the primary thread that holds Rilke's literary space together.

In a letter to the princess dated December 27, 1913, Rilke writes:

If God is reasonable, he will soon allow me to find a few rooms in the country where I can rave quite in my own way and where the Elegies may howl out of me at the moon from all sides, as much as they please. Add to this the possibility of taking long solitary walks, and finally, the human being, who like a beloved sister !!! (alas, alas) would look after the house and have no desire whatsoever or so much that she would ask nothing but to be there functioning and protecting at the border of the invisible. Such is the essence of my wishes for 1914, 15, 16, 17 and so forth.

But Rilke will have to wait until 1920 and Nanny for his wish to come true. In Nanny, Rilke finds the silent and invisible "sister" who manages his life from a distance, through letters, represented in person by a silent housekeeper. She has to see the chateau de Muzot only once or twice before taking action, and when Rilke moves in—more precisely, when she moves him in—he insists that she see it again:

How can you superintend Muzot in the same way as Berg if you don't know it at all? Just think of how complicated and painstaking it would be if I had to describe to you every single wish that comes to my mind during the course of the winter; on the other hand, if you had a well-informed *(mitwissend)* idea of Muzot, I could simply inscribe, as on a map, the point towards which you should turn your kind attention and care, and you would immediately understand how to solve this geographical exercise. *(October 17, 1921)*

Ideally, he should only have to point at whatever problem he has, without even a written explanation, in order to have it immediately resolved. Nanny Wunderly is a small miracle, the closest he can come to the ideal. Rilke can even count on her to communicate with his housekeeper—his messages going from Muzot to Muzot, via Winterthur, Switzerland—especially when the message requests her absolute silence. To tell her personally would be to open himself up to discussion, and he might as well let the whole world approach him. The housekeeper must not speak to him, but he cannot tell her so himself:

Dearest, if you should happen to write to Frida, to answer her statement of accounts, you could perhaps in passing allude to the fact that I have caught up with my correspondence, and that I soon will be immersed in a period of serious work, and you could remind her, as if it came entirely from you, that she should then *speak to me as little as possible:* not at the table, nor when she believes that I am not busy, and especially not when I return from my excursions, because I usually have something half-finished in my mind, which should not be interrupted nor troubled by her words. *(December 7, 1921)*

At first, when Rilke decides, after much hesitation, to move to Muzot, the housekeeper problem seems almost insurmountable. Nothing is harder than finding someone who is at once efficient—who knows how to do just about everything, especially cook (Rilke is, after all, used to living in a hotel or a chateau)—robust enough to handle some discomfort and the harsh climate, and also stupid enough for him not to have to think much about her. The problem arises most sharply in the case of Madame Schenk, a "demoted" dentist (according to Rilke), whom he decides not to hire because he fears he will pay too much attention to the fate of someone "who has some nobility" (October 7, 1921). Only a good, strapping country girl has no destiny.

In any case, the move to Muzot is far from smooth, and it brings out all of Rilke's centrifugal tendencies. Made available by Nanny Wunderly's cousin (W. Reinhart), the chateau must be renovated in order to be livable. Yet Rilke will agree to move there only if he can be free to change his mind at any point. He expects his patron to find him a space that he is free *not* to occupy, for which he owes her nothing, not even his presence in it. If W. Reinhart renovates Muzot, it must not be on Rilke's account. He hesitates for several weeks, "for fear of obligation" (July 15, 1921); for fear that another person will poison the space he is about to occupy by (morally) obliging him to stay there. No sooner has he made his decision (July 20, 1921) than he has a last change of mind. On July 25 he writes enthusiastically to

Nanny about the possiblity of spending the winter elsewhere (in a manor house in Kaiserstuhl) and spending only a few weeks at Muzot. This plan falls through, however, and Muzot becomes Rilke's last real home (also, to a certain extent, his first). It is perfectly symptomatic of Rilke's relationship to space, which will never be fully his own, even if he is given his own set of keys.

chapter two

What Words Lack

Debt

The letter writer in search of a separate space addresses others less in order to communicate than to exclude them and deny them complicity in an exchange. He rejects not only the other but also the possibility of any kind of partnership. Behind any particular other is always the Other: not an alter ego constructed in the image of the author, with whom he can identify, but a more general and different Other made up of all others (except those the letter writer knows personally); an Other who anonymously proves communication possible, who witnesses and guarantees the success of words. (I am using, of course, the distinction proposed by Lacan between the imaginary other and the symbolic Other, which he also sometimes defines as the "lieu de la convention signifiante,"[1] or the location of the law on which the existence of the speaking subject depends.)

Beyond the paradoxical questioning of an individual other, writers' letters frequently indicate a kind of defiance directed at the symbolic Other. The writer challenges the Other's law, or he challenges him as lawmaker; he refuses to become his subject. The Other must disappear (or become a barred Other) and where the law was, the letter writer's own desire must appear. The epistolary distance allows for repeated infractions of the law. It creates a form of rupture with the Other—a rupture, even a transgression or perversion of the law, which sometimes becomes the primary purpose of letter writing. Throughout history there have been countless illicit epistolary exchanges, conducted in jealous secrecy or in absolute confidentiality. Letters are a form of organized resistence to the Other, an attempt to liberate or reconquer a territory under enemy rule. The epistolary mode can be seen as a rupture with the *symbolic* as defined by Claude Lévi-Strauss and Lacan (most notably in the first *Ecrits*). Letters, more often than one thinks, attack social bonds and subvert conventions. The resulting failure of social ties probably constitutes the most fundamental intersection between letters and literary discourse. A poem and a letter are linked by their defiance of the symbolic; united they often form its greatest opposition.

Charles Baudelaire's letters are perhaps the most obvious example of this. Their embodiment of Baudelaire's financial debt and the paperwork it requires gives form and continuity to a legal infraction or transgression. His state of debt is far less a practical concern than it is the symptom of a defiant relationship with the Other, an incessant questioning of the symbolic.

From Flaubert's immobility to Baudelaire's hypermobility: he moves constantly, within Paris, from hotel to hotel without ever leaving a forwarding address, since he moves primarily to escape his growing number of debts and the creditors who are trying to track him down. Or sometimes simply because he has no money to pay his rent. His life is marked by an instability and fragility of lodging. Moving is for Baudelaire an imperious necessity long before it becomes one of the principal forces in his aesthetic (as in *Les foules*). He masters the art of escape and physical distance—all of which would not seem directly relevant to his correspondence save for the fact that his letters are almost exclusively concerned with debts. Whether the letters are addressed to his mother (his main correspondent), to his legal counsel Ancelle (engaged by his mother to prevent him from squandering his entire inheritance in a couple of years), to his publishers, or to any of his other many correspondents, they almost always concern money. He either asks for money, promises to repay it, acknowledges debts, explains the delays in payment or asks for extensions. The minute developments of debt define Baudelaire's daily rhythm, his basic pacing, and almost all of his relationships with others.

Baudelaire takes little pleasure in his letters. Nor is he involved in them as Kafka, Flaubert, or Proust were. No one has ever considered him an epistolary genius—his letters are prosaic and far from literary. They often seem to have been dashed off angrily in response to some emergency. They are pitiful, complaining, miserable, and in the end say only one thing: that he would be much happier if he didn't have to write them, if he owed nothing to anyone. But since, at the same time, he is constantly sinking further into debt, he has no choice in the matter. Debts must be handled, and can only be handled through letters. When Baudelaire's creditors try to enforce the law and insist on payment, letters create a sort of protective zone around him. They neutralize the law, allowing for what Kafka would have called an infinite postponement. Baudelaire, the letter writer, walks a tightrope. His letters officially recognize his debts without paying them. They cover (in the least financial meaning of the word) and disguise his infraction of the law; and they postpone the fulfillment of contracted agreements.

Letters are Baudelaire's counterfeit (the title of one of the texts in *Spleen de Paris*). He writes letters instead of paying his debts or, more fundamentally, to get out of paying them. The poet is a gambler and a speculator (sometimes with the devil as partner, as in "Le joueur généreux"). On one level, Baudelaire gets into debt *in order* to write, and in particular to make it known that he cannot pay his debts. Each letter forces him deeper and deeper into debt. How else to interpret his incredible obstinacy in the face of debt, his absolute refusal to settle his accounts and to "reform" his life? He never makes the least attempt to earn money and never completes any of the marketable novels or plays whose outlines repeatedly crop up in his letters. Because, as we know, as Baudelaire knows all too well, poetry and money belong to different worlds, and he did not become a poet for financial gain. On the contrary, he repeatedly affirms (if not in his letters, which at least *promise* some form of compensation) that poetry is a world apart from money and law. Baudelaire spends his life making it known that he is not where he owes it to himself to be, and that perhaps he is even better off where he is: like the founders of colonies or the missionaries described in *Les foules,* the blissful masses of this world cannot understand his superior happiness (the poem as a whole deals with his debt to the Other, to all others, to the crowds who, without knowing it, inspire the poet-wanderer).

Writing to get into debt, getting into debt in order to write: Baudelaire's correspondence begins this endless oscillation long before the least *financial* debt is incurred (hence my decision to treat Baudelaire's financial problems as a symptom of something deeper). At the age of twelve, he is already overwhelmed by his unpaid debt to others. The letters he writes from Lyon to his older half-brother Alphonse are full of confessions, apologies for his bad conduct and his laziness at school, justifications, promises for the future. Even when he has no bad behavior to apologize for, he can always excuse himself for having taken so long to write, a fault that demands further explanations, justifications, and promises: "You scold me for not writing you (it's true, I confess, I have been lazy) . . . To prove to you how much affection I have for my older brother, I promise to write him as often as I have time" (December 15, 1832).

A few weeks earlier, Charles wrote to Alphonse: "I am delighted at your being appointed *deputy judge*" (November 9, 1832). It is not quite clear what absent, silent father Alphonse and others after him—Ancelle or Aupick, Baudelaire's stepfather—are "deputies" for (Charles has only one picture of his real father, but he keeps it all his life). And the charm Charles finds in his relationship with Alphonse seems strange when one thinks of the rather cool reception he gives to later authority figures. His letters to Ancelle, for example, are always a strange mixture of contempt and hostility, despite the occasional attempts to charm him. As for General Aupick, Charles is tempted to take advantage of the 1848 uprisings to kill him.

Baudelaire also writes to his mother and stepfather from his school in Lyon, but he never receives the grades that would allow him to make an excursion or come home for a visit. His poor grades ensure his continued separation from his family, and his relationship with them is a constant rupture that his letters struggle to overcome. But it is already too late:

> I'm writing to try to persuade you that there is still some hope of pulling me out of the state that causes you such suffering. I know that as soon as Mother reads the beginning of this letter, she'll say: "I don't believe it's still possible," and Father will say the same. But I'm not going to let that discourage me; you want to punish me for my follies by not coming to see me at the college, but come one last time to give me some good advice and to encourage me . . . You're beginning to believe that I'm ungrateful; indeed you're convinced of it, perhaps. How can I make you believe the very opposite? I know how to do it: by getting down to work straightaway. *But whatever I do the time I've spent in laziness, forgetful of what I owed you, will always be a blot. (February 25, 1834; my italics)*

A promising beginning in life. At thirteen, the ungrateful youth is already marked by a stain that nothing will remove, by a debt that will prevent him from ever returning to his mother. The debate always seems to circle around his mother (perhaps because of a conscious effort on her part). Later, as Philippe Bonnefis has remarked, no matter whom Baudelaire addresses immediately, she is always his ultimate correspondent, his primary creditor.[2] Moreover, when she forces a legal executor on her son to prevent him from spending what is left of the inheritance from his father, she turns her son's debts to her advantage. Payment of his inheritance is blocked and, for more than twenty years, she pays the debts that Baudelaire continues to contract, thus becoming his only real creditor. Baudelaire later comments on the ambiguous nature of this act: "How on earth do you succeed in always being for your son the very opposite of a *friend,* except in matters of money, and even then provided—and this is what reveals what an absurd, and yet at the same time generous, character you have—that such matters do not affect you" (April 1, 1861).

Madame Aupick is both absurd and generous. It is as if she had condemned her son to debt from the moment of his birth (or perhaps because of his birth); as if, in advance, he owed her all he would ever get and all he would ever become. Charles's identity is negotiated in the shadow of maternal influence. His mother establishes herself as the Other, a primordial creditor whom it is impossible to pay back, under whose influence the creditors to come can only multiply. She gives her son no choice but to live in a state of permanent transgression.

Baudelaire's first debt is lost forever in the eternal night, in the incalculable, where nothing will ever suffice to pay it back (how can you put a figure on what you owe your mother?). Whatever he does, the debt will only increase. He thus works with perverse determination not to do anything, not to get a job, not to go anywhere, not to be anyone but a subject in constant movement, transitory, scattered. The only way to stay out of debt—to his mother or anyone else—is to refuse to settle his identity, to offer nothing but an account of incalculable insignificance.

The first rule of the game for Baudelaire is to avoid owing his mother an identity or situation that he would have to account for to the Other. But with no real place in society, he is condemned to live outside the law and to count on his mother all the more. They maintain a kind of infernal complicity; he must own nothing that he could possibly owe to someone else. He rushes to spend all that he has (or all that he can spend before his mother hires legal counsel to stop him).[3] He values luxury, calm, pleasure, laziness, and beauty; he becomes a dandy and lives beyond his means. Most important, Baudelaire carries this attitude into his poetry, which constantly represents itself as being outside the realms of price and value, a pure infraction of law and obligation. Beyond the immediate charms of sensuality, behind the "correspondences" and identifications, the seductions and pleasures, the dreams of absolute wealth or immortality, what Baudelaire wants most is to evade his debt and to seduce or pervert the Other. Everything he writes is marked by a defiance of the Other. His poems, as in *Paris Spleen,* are inhabited by gamblers, speculators, and counterfeiters, or describe gratuitous acts and crimes.

Baudelaire struggles not to own anything he might eventually have to return to someone else. He dreams of a space removed from the world of exchange and debt. Once in debt, he turns it against himself by going ever deeper into it and finds, in this fall, the possibility of a poetic experience or, rather, a poetic *escape* from his impossible situation. Baudelaire's work is almost a by-product of his debt, of the state of transgression he maintains throughout his life, which can be defined in terms of this transgression (there is nothing more unreliable than to speculate on what Baudelaire might have written without his financial problems). Seen in this light, his correspondence is the necessary antipode to his work and exposes a certain truth about it. The letters reinstate the contractual or expressive framework that his poetry breaks down. They tabulate the symbolic cost of Baudelaire's poetic evasions. On one side of the desk, we have Baudelaire the dreamer-aesthete, the great melancholic; on the other, Baudelaire the debtor to the Other. Most of his letters are written as debtor. In all of them, he is haunted by the Other and the desire to be free.

Contrary to appearances, Baudelaire's correspondence is a "poetic" necessity. Through it, he maintains the paradoxical character of his subjective position, which is also the position he writes from. By refusing to settle his accounts with the Other, he prevents himself from disappearing, from being nowhere. He can exist, at least, in his promises for the future. For over thirty years, Baudelaire sends his mother countless letters acknowledging a wide variety of debts: "I ought to take into account that in seventeen years you gave or lent me many thousands of francs, and it is fully time, not only not to go on borrowing from you, but also to repay you" (December 15, 1859). Or: "What can I say but what you could so easily guess; that I am very bored, that I think how happy I should be with you, that I very often wonder how I can make amends for all I have to make amends for, and that I am terrified by the greatness of my task, etc.?" (September 3, 1865).

From Lyon to Paris, from Brussels to Honfleur, the message is the same, and so is the debt—all the harder to repay since it requires not only a reimbursement of borrowed money but the acquisition of fame and success, the incalculable: "But I hope, one day, to pay it all back to you; don't think that I mean especially and simply the money; *I want to give you back more than your money*" (December 5, 1847). Already at sixteen, Baudelaire dreams of a success that would satisfy and delight his mother before she dies: "When I begin to think of the enormous number of benefits I owe you, I see that the only way to repay you is by satisfying your vanity, by my successes. But my poor mother, if nature failed to make me capable of satisfying you, if I'm of too limited intelligence to please your ambitions, you'll die before I've been able to repay you even to a small extent for all the trouble you've given yourself" (June 27, 1838). And several days later: "My dear mother, if you knew how I long to enjoy your company and to bring you honor before you die!" (July 2, 1838).

He is starting rather early, considering that his mother will live for another thirty-three years (dying four years after him). But he should have begun at birth, or even earlier: all his life he has been just a little too late, which is why he never fully succeeds in doing what is needed to pay off the debts and satisfy his mother. There is nothing less per-formative than Baudelaire's promises to his mother. Words work only for those who believe in the symbolic realm, and they take him farther and farther away from the possibility of action. The discrepancy be-tween what his letters promise and what he performs is never fully resolved. Minor details always get in the way, preventing Charles from coming home to Madame Aupick. For years he is on the verge of joining her at Honfleur, but he is always kept in Paris at the last minute by an urgent business matter: "To have happiness only a step away, almost within my grasp and not to be able to seize it! And to know that not only am I to be happy but also that I'll be giving happiness to someone who deserves it" (February 19, 1858). A certain distance, minimal but absolute, will always prevent his happiness from coinciding with his mother's—it is the least amount of air and space necessary to allow him to breathe, to write, to confess his guilt: "If you knew on what thoughts I feed, the fear of dying before having done what I have to do, the fear of your dying before I have made you completely happy, you, the one being with whom I can live at peace, without tricks, without lies" (March 26, 1860).

"To live at peace, without tricks, without lies"—and without ever breaking his promises, as if his debts had been paid. This is the utopia Baudelaire envisions to ward off the fears he seems to feed on, the imminent catastrophes or definitive breaks. He writes again and again in order to neutralize and delay the inevitable separation from his mother, which he thinks of constantly. During the last years of his life, this fear takes hold of him. He and his mother race against the clock to see who will die first of the wounds they inflict on each other (both knowing full well that the winner of the race will never survive the loser):

> We're obviously destined to love one another, to end our lives as honestly and gently as possible. And yet, in the awful circumstances in which I find myself, I'm convinced that one of us will kill the other, and that the end will come through each of us killing the other. After my death, you won't go on living: that's clear. I'm the only thing you live for. After your death, especially if you were to die through a shock I'd caused, I'd kill myself—that's beyond doubt. *(May 6, 1861)*

Don't die or I'll kill myself; don't kill me or you'll die. Madame Aupick and her son live only through and for the debts they believe they owe each other. Baudelaire's whole being is reduced to his debt, to what he knows perfectly well he will never pay back. His mother's disappearance would threaten his own existence. His letters try to ward off the threat, to prevent the dissolution of the diabolical pact that rules his life, and to keep alive the phantom of a law that is constantly broken: "you'll understand me perfectly when I tell you that I beg you *to stay in good health, look after yourself well, live as long as you can,* and *grant me your indulgence a little longer*" (December 31, 1863). Don't die. Let me go on owing you everything and never paying you back. Let me be always at fault, never coming back to you. For Baudelaire, no other form of existence seems possible.

When he finally returns from Brussels to Honfleur, to his mother's house, he is on the point of dying, ill, aphasic, deprived of the ability to speak and to make promises he cannot keep. His debt lasts only as long as his life. What more could his mother ask, having given him life and speech? He comes back to her, undoubtedly at great cost, but bringing with him the rest of his blocked inheritance, which will again allow Madame Aupick control over his financial affairs. He comes back to her, body and assets, to pay back the debt incurred by his poetry. Poetry has always been, for her, an investment her son tricked her into making and through which he has managed to evade the law she tried to enforce. Baudelaire's oeuvre is "capital" whose interest his mother will not realize until much later, too late. But could she have done otherwise with work that was specifically intended to be incomprehensible to her?

> There is a more serious state than physical suffering and that's the fear of watching as there wastes away, falls into jeopardy, and disappears in this horrible existence with all its upheavals, the admirable poetic gift, the clarity of ideas and the power of hope which alone make up my true wealth. My dear mother, you are so utterly unaware of what a poet's life is like that you probably won't make much sense of this argument . . . And I believe that my personality is highly valuable, I won't say more valuable than others, but valuable enough for me. *(December 20, 1855)*

Baudelaire spends his life defying the Other, producing hundreds of letters to express his defiance, to affirm that he has not been understood and that his most valuable qualities are priceless.

Before the Law

Vor dem Gesetz: there is, at the heart of all of Kafka's stories and novels, a law whose definition escapes you but which you cannot escape. It summons you, it arrests you, without warning. Like Josef K., one minute you are preparing breakfast and the next you are involved in a trial. As in the monstrous machine of "The Penal Colony," this law can be written out in bodies; it can crush them with the same mad ferocity with which it will eventually destroy itself. Or it can be impossible to find. You can knock on every door, search every castle, exhaust yourself seducing watchmen and their mistresses, haunting the antechambers, the chancelleries, calling, writing: no answer ever arrives and no connection is possible. The law holds you as strongly with its absence as with its presence. You are as indebted to it as Baudelaire was to his creditors, but it owes you nothing.

This question runs through Kafka's letters to Felice Bauer: how can you escape the law or, more precisely, how can you escape it without annihilating yourself? The escape itself carries the threat of destruction. How can you exist and not be subject to the law? Suicide is one solution (the idea haunts Kafka as it did Baudelaire), madness is another (he often feels it coming on), but these are both forms of annihilation: you cannot survive them. You can also play dead, hide in your hole or burrow, but then time becomes the enemy. The Other will always find you sooner or later; hence the growing anguish of the beast hiding in its *Bau*. Not to mention the opposite risk: if you play dead long enough, you will end up really dead. That is perhaps exactly what an indifferent law wants; it has all the time in the world and thinks only of itself.

How to escape from the law without destroying oneself, and how to return from such an exile? Kafka, more systematically than Baudelaire, chooses letters as his means. His letters are an endless homecoming, just as he is a permanent fiancé. The two come down to almost the same thing, since his relationship to the symbolic is centered on the question of marriage. For Kafka the first law to be avoided is the one that can force him to give his word once and for all, to name the object of his desire, to be recognized as a man and to recognize the other as his wife. His letters to Felice avoid that moment; they infinitely prolong the engagement and postpone the public declaration of their relationship. Like Baudelaire's letters, they combine a gesture of allegiance to the law (the repeated promise of an alliance to come) with a gesture of subversion. They slyly pervert the projected union by refusing to speak of it. The engagement they bear witness to is based on the absence of the other. Kafka writes to Felice about marriage, but demands secrecy. The cellar-dweller needs only a shadow desire. To make a public declaration (a true marriage), he would have to leave his cellar, step into the light, and then, logically, both the desire and the cellar-dweller would cease to exist: "Can you understand this, Felice, if only from a distance? I have a definite feeling that through marriage, *through the union, through the dissolution* of this nothingness *(dieses Nichtigen)* that I am, I shall perish, and not alone but with my wife, and that the more I love her the swifter and the more terrible it will be" (July 10, 1913).

Marriage would be a dissolution of the nothing (or the insignificant, unnamed thing) that Kafka the insect is trying to be. Similarly, it would cause the disappearance of the nothing that Felice represents— courted as she was for her striking "insignificance." Marriage would destroy the semblance of existence created by letters that Kafka favors over all other forms. It is better to be a ghost and to eat nothing like the *Hungerkünstler,* the hunger artist whose fast is an attraction at the town fair, than to be crushed by the law. Anything rather than lose the intimacy with absence that letters allow him.

This is, of course, interpretation. There is nothing in the letters to indicate directly that Kafka began his correspondence in order to challenge a law that was both eluding and threatening him. In fact, his writing also embodies a dream of reconciliation with the law, a well-intentioned law (symbolized by Palestine). But he places his beliefs, his hope, and his despair in letters, and they choose for him, perhaps in spite of him. In any case, the price exacted for his allegiance to letters is a heavy one. It becomes a classical form of hell with eternal torments and tortures: you cannot attach yourself to an indeterminate, nameless reality and not pay a price. The correspondence itself becomes a form of torture: "God, it really is about time to ease the pressure, and there surely isn't a girl who has been loved as I love you, and been tortured as I find it necessary to torture you" (July 10, 1913). "And the worst of it is that again letters follow from both sides dealing exclusively with the writing of letters— empty, time-wasting letters, secretly no more than accounts of the torture it is, or rather can be, to carry on a correspondence" (to Grete Bloch, November 18, 1913). With letters you start by promising Palestine, and you eventually find yourself toiling next to Sisyphus or Tantalus, suffering through all their infinite torments and boredom, or beside their Kafkaesque brother, the hunter Gracchus, the dead man who misses the entrance to hell and wanders from port to port in his funeral barque.

In Kafka's life, Felice seems to occupy the position of what is sometimes called the *thing* in psychoanalysis (the Freudian *Ding*),[4] a role first occupied by the mother. A primordial thing, with no name, the source of a radically forbidden pleasure and recognized as such by the anguish her approach inspires. On July 10, 1913, after their first engagement, Kafka writes:

> After all, we have never been as united as we are now; this Yes on both sides has tremendous power. But I am held back by what is almost a command from heaven; an apprehension that cannot be appeased; everything that used to be of the greatest importance to me—my health, my small income, my miserable disposition, all this for which there would be some justification—vanishes, is as nothing compared to this apprehension, and seems to be used only as a pretext.

Again, a quasi-theoretical description of a battle: as the ultimate shield against forbidden pleasure, a pure anguish (one of the joys of the superego) falls on you like a commandment from heaven whenever the pretexts, the resistance, and the misleading symptoms disappear. The closer you come to the thing, the greater the resistance. Love, according to Kafka, is an endless obstacle course: "I do not believe that the battle for any woman in any fairy tale has been fought harder and more desperately than the battle for you within myself—from the beginning, over and over again, and perhaps forever" (October 19, 1916; this passage was used as an epigraph in the original edition of the letters). The battle is controlled and paced by the epistolary exchange, which alone can support it and make it last. The letters hold Felice in the position of the *thing,* forbidden and invisible as long as possible.

A correspondence with the *thing* holds off the threat contained in its actual presence but does not actually dissolve it by declaring it to the Other. To become officially, publicly engaged would relieve Kafka of the *thing*—now made specific by a name, a promise—and the anguish it causes. But it would also require him to give up the refuge of letters:

> And from now on don't write to me so much. A hectic correspondence is a sign that something is wrong. Peace requires no letters. Nothing in itself will change through my becoming your fiancé in the eyes of the whole world, but at least it is the signal for the end of all outward expressions of doubts and fears. Consequently there is no further need for as many letters; there is need only for the utmost regularity in writing, a regularity calculated to a hair's breadth. You will be amazed what a poor though punctual letter writer I shall turn into once I am your fiancé. There will be increasingly stronger ties, compared to which letters will be ridiculous. *(August 15, 1913)*

If Kafka were to get engaged, and (worse) to marry, it would mean the end of his freedom from the law and the destruction of the perverse position letters have allowed him. And it would definitely cool his interest in the relationship. "Come soon, let's get married, let's put an end to it," he later writes to Felice (April 22, 1914), to whom the idea of marrying Kafka no longer seems so appealing. Understandably, considering that Felice naturally sees marriage more as a beginning than an ending.

To evade the law that commands him to give his word and declare his position in person, Kafka instead marries himself to letters—and his correspondents with him—for better or (more often) for worse. On the night of December 31, 1912, he writes to Felice: "But the finest 13 won't prevent me from drawing you, my dearest, closer, closer, closer to me. Where are you at this moment? From whose company am I drawing you away?" Kafka's New Year's wishes for 1913 describe his resolutions and plans for the year: to tear Felice away from her friends and family, from society, and from the Other, just as he has extricated himself. Inversely, he wants to exclude the Other, in all its forms, from their epistolary relationship: "Come here, dearest! No one is to be between us, no one around us" (February 12–13, 1913).

Kafka's letters attempt to break the bonds that tie him to the Other, especially his parents, to whom he owes his name and his existence. They, more than anyone or anything else, embody the pressures of the law that stifles him and infringes on his private space. He has to cross their bedroom passing the unmade bed, which makes him nauseous—"it is as though my birth had not been final"—to get to his own:

> I have always looked upon my parents as persecutors; until about a year ago I was indifferent to them and perhaps to the world at large, as some kind of lifeless thing, but I see now it was only suppressed fear, worry, and unhappiness. All parents want to do is drag one down to them, back to the old days from which one longs to free oneself and escape; they do it out of love, of course, and that's what makes it so horrible. *(November 21, 1912)*

His letters are often written less to Felice than against his parents, as a secret from them (hence Kafka's rage when his mother goes through his pockets). He tries to invalidate his parents in writing, the way one invalidates a contract, and the claim of the Other they represent.

Kafka uses his contact with Felice as a refuge from his family, as he explains in the following letter (a charming family portrait, probably just as reassuring a document for his future wife to read as *The Metamorphosis*):

> Yesterday afternoon when everyone foregathered here after my parents' return and, led by my father in a positive frenzy, the whole family, while playing with this child, lost themselves in the nethermost regions of sexuality, I felt as revolted as if I'd been condemned to live in a sty . . . But there of course, in the midst of it, sat my poor mother who has never had the time or ever learned how to keep her body in proper shape, and who is now bloated and bent from work and giving birth to 6 children . . . there sat my eldest sister who but two years ago was still a young girl, yet whose body, after producing a couple of children, is now really beginning, more from neglect and ignorance than from lack of time, to resemble that of my mother—and there she sat, her figure bulging out of some extraordinary corset. And on closer scrutiny, even my middle sister is showing signs of looking like the eldest.—*Dearest, how I sought refuge with you! (June 23, 1913; my italics—I quote this passage mainly for its conclusion.)*

He longs to escape from his family, from the father who cannot control himself and these women, mothers and sisters whose impossible bodies just get fatter and more and more obtrusive. Letters provide an escape route from the symbolic and the small family events that hold it together, as Deleuze and Guattari have shown,[5] protecting Kafka from the law and its Oedipal figures. His escape route leads to no one, nowhere—a fact Felice is required to register over and over again. Kafka depends on a fundamental and necessary miscommunication; he communicates with Felice as if with someone who exists outside the law and never, as she expects (legitimately, at first), to make an actual contract.

Kafka's epistolary writing denounces the Other and its privileged representatives. Nothing is harder for Kafka than to communicate with a father, his own or Felice's: "My letter to your father is not yet finished, or rather it was finished several times, but each time quite unsuitable" (May 23, 1913). Letters to fathers are never sent or end up at the bottom of a drawer: "for 4 days—the letter to your father has been lying, completed, in my drawer" (August 24, 1913). And when Kafka finally does write to Carl Bauer, it is less to introduce himself than to confess his epistolary crimes: "I have deluded your daughter with my letters; as a rule I have not meant to deceive her (although sometimes I have, because I loved her and love her, and have been terribly aware of our incompatibility), and perhaps by doing just this, I blinded her" (August 28, 1913).

Before even officially becoming Felice's fiancé (and most likely in an attempt to avoid it), he announces to Carl Bauer that he has betrayed his daughter by engaging her in a shameful epistolary exchange. Kafka confesses to Bauer as if to a judge who will pass sentence, who will declare him an "outlaw." His letter ends with the following line: "Well, now we are three. You be the judge!" It is impossible for Kafka to pass from a clandestine, seductive twosome to a relationship sanctioned by a father, the third party par excellence. Instead he stubbornly conducts his own trial.[6]

This exclusion of any kind of mediation or third party is also a refusal of the Other. But by the fall of 1913 (a year after the beginning of their liaison), things have already gone very wrong between the epistolary lovers. They need a mediator, and the role is filled by Felice's friend, Grete Bloch. Not much notice has been paid to one of the most surprising aspects of the "letters to Felice": more than a quarter of them are addressed to Grete, who takes over the position of the now silent fiancée. It begins after Kafka's return from Berlin, where Grete arranged his meeting with Felice: "Dear Fräulein Bloch, I returned from Berlin last night, I am writing to you before writing to F. This trip was largely your doing, and you were responsible; I can thank you only by telling you about it" (November 10, 1913). From the first letter written to her, Grete takes precedence over Felice. The epistolary journey erases the real and miserable journey. From this point on, Grete spends more nights on the exchange than Felice does (Kafka writes very little to her): "Dear Fräulein Bloch, now I am robbing you of your nights, am conscious of your sympathy which exceeds both my imagination and my faculties, bask in it for days on end, yet fail to answer . . . By the way, I haven't written once to F. since my visit, nor have I heard from her. Isn't the latter rather strange?" (November 18, 1913).

It is strange, but true, and the whole process begins again with Grete. Only the correspondence itself seems to count—with the same complaints and worries when a response is slow to arrive, the same anxious calculation of postal collection and delivery times, the same demands for regularity: "Dear Fräulein Grete, it would have been a good thing, after all, if we had decided on set times for our letters. In that case I wouldn't have ever-recurring thoughts." (March 12, 1914). The correspondence between Kafka and Grete does not begin, as a means of resolving the problems with Felice, but as an alternative to that dead-end relationship. Where Kafka had sought refuge from his family in Felice, he now turns to Grete to recover from the more and more painful meetings with his fiancée—who has begun, like his family, to embody the law: "If there was any comfort in these two days, it was the thought of you, your loyalty and honesty" (March 2, 1914; written after a particularly sinister weekend in Berlin with Felice). Grete is thus, little by little and probably against her will,[7] transformed from intermediary to principal participant in a correspondence that quickly becomes an end in itself. Kafka soon demands silence and secrecy from the person who began as a mediator. His correspondence with Grete becomes more and more hidden from Felice, and his relationship with Felice becomes more and more hidden from Grete:

You may not yet realize as I do that although our respective relationships with F. cannot be eliminated—for that they are too strong, perhaps indissoluble—they at least no longer form the most important part in our own relationship; so that I may well pass the whole affair over in silence when words fail me, but that this should not prevent the hands we held out to each other in friendship from being clasped as firmly as ever. *(March 12, 1914)*

Grete is the ideal correspondent because her role as intermediary excludes any real alliance. Her attempts to bring the fiancés closer together preclude any question of marriage for herself. Her role as intermediary allows Kafka to turn her into a confidante, to require secrecy (how could she repeat to Felice all the negative things he says about her?), and to involve her in another epistolary seduction, which is for Kafka a form of infidelity or perversion. There is definitely something diabolical in Kafka's epistolary methods.

The charm of a postal ménage-à-trois: on one side the fiancée who doesn't want to write anymore, on the other a captivated intermediary who has taken over the correspondence. The circle could go on forever, and Kafka probably would have liked that. When his engagement to Felice finally comes about (perhaps only because he has stopped smothering her with letters), he immediately writes to reassure Grete:

> But there is one thing I can't tell you soon enough and that's this: Our relationship, which for me at least holds delightful and altogether indispensable possibilities, is in no way changed by my engagement or my marriage. Is this a fact, and will it remain so? I repeat, in case it hasn't been made clear already: All this is independent of anything that I and F. (so far as I, the bridegroom, can say this) owe to you in our affairs. *(April 14, 1914)*

The engagement changes nothing. The correspondence must go on and does go on for several more weeks, just long enough for Grete to grasp her strange correspondent's aversion to a marriage with Felice and to understand her own role in the plot. The correspondence lasts until she too has had enough and backs out of her position as confidante by telling Felice everything.

Kafka never finds a middle ground between seduction by letters and its trial by letters. These are two sides of the same relationship to the law, as his triumphant letter to Grete shows. It is as if the whole correspondence with Grete existed only to bring about this final moment of denunciation to Felice:

> My dear Fräulein Grete, that is certainly a very unambiguous letter. It looks as though I have convinced you at last. Sooner than F., for we have known each other only since November, whereas it took almost a year to convince F. for the first time . . . The sole object of our relationship, Fräulein Grete (although on a basis of friendship which I hope cannot be shaken by any possible revelation), was to convince you. *(July 3, 1914)*

In the last paragraph of the same letter, Kafka writes: "Incidentally, today is my birthday, so quite fortuitously your letter acquires a special solemnity." Felice's fiancé celebrates his rebirth as a pariah, his trickery exposed, summoned to a kind of family court at the Askanischer Hof in Berlin, where the end of the engagement will be officially announced. This of course ends the correspondence with Grete, as it does the correspondence with Felice (the letters still to come are just a protracted arrangement of the ending). Grete's mediation has failed, as has all mediation. The law comes into play only when Kafka arranges his exemption from it. A few days later, he begins writing *The Trial*: "Someone must have been telling lies about Joseph K., for without having done anything wrong he was arrested one fine morning." Happy Birthday, dear Franz . . . . .

Kafka's relationship to Grete Bloch, the intermediary, is also a relationship to the *word* and, more generally, to language, the cloth from which all conventions are cut. For Kafka as writer in the making, this is undoubtedly the most important element. His correspondence with Felice is a systematic subversion of language and speech—it short-circuits all communicative value that language might have, distracting it, like Grete, from its true mediating function. Letters about letters continue the flow of letters written in a blocked language that circles endlessly back to itself.

Kafka transports Felice from her circle of family and friends to a shameful intimacy which requires the sacrifice of her social impulses (all that makes her exist for others, outside of the correspondence). He places her in a no-man's-land where language is neutralized, where speech has no relation to action, and all that is required is a reply, an exchange of words. Yet, on another level, Kafka works aggressively to avoid this possibility: "What I am writing today is not an answer to your letter; perhaps that answer shall be in tomorrow's letter, possibly not until the following day's" (October 23, 1912). "God, I have still so many things to tell you, so many questions to answer, and I have come to the end, and besides, it's now 3 o'clock. Well, more tomorrow" (November 21, 1912). But tomorrow will bring a new letter and not enough time to answer it. The letters are so numerous and frequent that they cannot *correspond*. Questions and answers circle between Prague and Berlin like trains that pass in the night, on parallel tracks. It is always too late or too early to answer anything specific, and the letters fall definitively out of sync, fulfilling Kafka's desire to produce something indecipherable: "Once again I haven't answered anything, but answers have to be given orally; writing makes things indecipherable" (November 17, 1912). Fundamentally, Kafka does not want to answer or to be answered (even when the rate of letters slows sufficiently to allow it). The acts of reading and writing must not form an exchange: no answers, no questions, just a means of listening simply and disinterestedly to the other. "Felice, I don't want any answers to my letters; I want to hear about you, only about you" (April 10, 1913).

It is not even clear that he intends his letters to be read. "By the way, can you read my writing? A somewhat belated question" (January 22–23, 1913). It takes more than three months (and several hundred pages of letters) for Kafka to ask Felice if his writing is legible, in the most literal meaning of the word. In the meantime he repeatedly warns her against reading his letters and urges her not to: "Felice, I announce that this is one of those letters I wrote about recently, that should be torn up when you reach the second or third sentence. Now is the moment, Felice, tear it up; it is also my moment for not writing it, but alas, you will read it, as surely as I shall write it" (November 26, 1912). Don't read, don't torture yourself. Rest, sleep instead: "Tired, you are sure to be tired, my Felice, when you pick up this letter, and I must make an effort to write clearly to spare your sleepy eyes. Wouldn't you rather leave the letter unread for the moment, lie back, and go on sleeping for a few more hours after this week of noise and rush?" (November 30, 1912).

The letters to Felice fall more or less into two categories: those that Kafka does not manage to write and those that he should not write. The letters in both groups are marked by a disqualification and rejection of their content. They are prefaced either by "don't read this because it's not what I mean" or "don't read this because I mean it." (Kafka leaves a narrow margin of possibility for Felice, who does not seem particularly interested in abnormal behavioral studies.) This double bind forms a kind of paralysis or block.[8] In the face of all these disclaimers, Felice must find it impossible to respond or to become any kind of partner in an exchange.

One could say that the paralysis, fatigue, and monotony that Kafka inspires in Felice also appear in his language itself. His letters take all the power out of language, prevent any kind of real communication (*mitteilen,* the German word, also signifies a kind of sharing). They destroy its credibility and exhaust its possibilities, particularly the logical and argumentative possibilities (Kafka loves legal reasoning). He pieces together argument after argument to persuade Felice—but to do what? To break off the relationship? To marry him? He does not really know himself. The theorems and pleas he develops in place of compliments become almost an end in themselves. One no longer knows what he wants, and no longer wants to know. While the letters to Felice can be overwhelming, they end up inspiring a kind of nausea; they become numbing, hypnotic. Go to sleep, go to sleep, don't bother reading this.

Not even Kafka knows what he wants. All he understands and is interested in is the failure of language to work as an intermediary: "I cannot comfort anyone, because words fail me" (February 19–20, 1913). And the impossibility of answering for his words: "but I am driven by this feeling of anxiety in the midst of my lethargy, and I write, or fear I may at any moment write, irresponsible things. The wrong sentences lie in wait about my pen, twine themselves around its point, and are dragged along into the letters" (February 18–19, 1913).

Later, in one of the last letters to Felice, he explains: "I am a mendacious creature; for me it is the only way to maintain an even keel, my boat is fragile" (September 30 or October 1, 1917). This mendacious creature who performs in Kafka's letters also appears in his texts and novels. He is Joseph K. from *The Trial* and K. from *The Castle,* whose exhausting arguments are nothing compared to Kafka's epistolary ones. He appears too in the secondary characters, who are just as deceitful. Misunderstanding follows misunderstanding, and conversations have no relation to reality. Kafka's great stories are based on this mendacious creature, woven from the lying thread of language itself: enigmatic, indecipherable, uninterpretable (hence the hundreds of different critical interpretations of his work). His fiction testifies to the powerlessness and inadequacy of words—as if Kafka had to acknowledge and record, somewhere, the destruction of language that his letters worked so hard to effect.

The Gambler

A language that is ambiguous, paralyzed, nonfunctional, words that are not kept: from Prague to Paris, the forms are different but the stakes are the same. Like Kafka, Proust works methodically toward a destruction of the symbolic. This attack takes root, as for Kafka, in his correspondence. He regularly uses letters to cover his tracks and disguise his wishes, an octopus disappearing in a cloud of ink: "Don't take my request to see you too literally. Since it would be perhaps very difficult to realize and is perhaps just a whim on my part" (to L. Gautier-Vignal, January 7, 1915). A typical letter: he writes without wanting to be taken literally, without wanting his requests to be fulfilled, without wanting a true correspondence.

Proust the letter writer follows an aesthetic of nonreception. He sometimes finds it painful even to receive a letter because it will require an answer: "It's not 'sporting' of you to have replied to me. Don't do it again or I shall stop writing to you" (to Madame Straus, May 7, 1905). He empties language of its communicative potential, wearing it out like Kafka, making it say first one thing and then the opposite until it loses all meaning. To examine fully the extent of this activity, we should read (as Deleuze and Guattari have done)[9] two letters to the young man to whom Proust has offered a secretarial position—and about whom he is clearly having second thoughts:

> I repeat, to leave your position for one with me where you would have nothing to do (not even anything uninteresting, because I wouldn't have the courage to dictate to you what I could dictate so much faster to this typist) would be a pure absurdity. But if you think otherwise, you are free to decide what you want, and if you decide to come, don't write again, send a telegram to say that you are coming immediately, and if possible by a train arriving around ten o'clock in the evening or in the late afternoon, or after dinner, but not too late and not before two o'clock in the afternoon, because I would like to see you before you see anyone. I am explaining all this in case you come, but I hope that you will agree with my opinion. *(mid-July 1911)*

You are free to come and meet me. But if you do come, it's not because I asked you to, and you mustn't come at the wrong time. I will have nothing to do with it, will not be responsible for anything. He might as well say that if the meeting does take place, it will be the result, if not of a miracle, then of pure chance: "While just the idea of you leaving something for this vague secretarial position which has no interest for you seems crazy, I will tell you, *on the off chance,* and while wholeheartedly hoping that you will not consider it for a minute, what the job would consist of—so that you don't imagine that it is I who don't want to have you around" (early July 1911; my italics).

Nothing that happens should be premeditated. Only the unforeseen and unplanned can actually take place. Proust avoids any kind of contract or agreement, whether he is bound by it or is binding someone else. Marcel versus Mauss: he is generous, he gives presents, but only unexpectedly and confidentially, almost anonymously so that no one can give him anything back: "I am allowing myself the pleasure of sending your daughters the small objects we spoke of . . . I would prefer it if no one knew that it was me who sent these modest trifles to your adorable daughters. If someone were to ask who had sent them and if you answered that it was an old friend of yours whom no one knows and who has been almost dead for years, you would do me a great honor" (to Charles d'Alton, October 1911). And he finds it impossible to receive anything (in all senses of the term). If you give him a present, he'll send it back immediately, for fear of being tied to you. Offer him the use of your villa and he'll refuse it, not wanting to be indebted to you for the space he occupies, or else he'll insist on paying for it: "I didn't even stay in my *brother's* villa in Louvenciennes because he refused to rent it to me" (to A. Nahmias, September 28 or 29, 1915). Give him a painting and he'll be uncomfortable and insist on paying for it: "I made up my mind to send back to you this masterpiece which I cannot accept, which in my house, where not even the shutters are opened, would find itself in a disagreeable prison . . . I should be unhappy with this beautiful object. But if you allow me to pay the ransom for its captivity, never will a marvellously beautiful slave have received greater respect and adoration" (to Paul Helleu, late February 1908). He tries to buy the gift in order to make it his own possession, empty of all associations and debts to others, to be guarded as jealously as a slave or prisoner.

As with the painting, Marcel pays a high price—her dresses, his yacht—in order to keep Albertine captive. He is a jealous jailer and will pay any amount to make her his own, to take her away from the Other. In this way he hopes also to stop desiring her, to stop demanding an explanation of her perverse pleasures that he tortures himself imagining. He will pay whatever it takes not to form his own questions about her, to cut her off from language and reduce her to the pure state she enters in sleep—incapable of producing misleading signals or fooling her guardian. He dreams of a silent Albertine kept secret from the world and permanently asleep.

As it is, words fail with her; they cannot express a truth that lasts. When she speaks or when Marcel speaks to her, lies, tricks and pretenses multiply, words ring false, language is derailed. Albertine the fugitive: from domestic scene to seduction, from conversation to interrogation, language falls to pieces around her. She tires it out, like Marcel who exhausts himself imagining explanation after explanation without ever really knowing the cause of his mistress' disappearance. Who is Albertine and what does she want? Proust writes hundreds of pages to avoid answering this question. The truth can never be expressed in words. All that remains is Marcel's fatigue, his long quest for information abandoned. One would guess that his "correspondents" (the "young man" and others) would also give up in the end, tired of receiving such contradictory messages. Before he projects himself into Albertine, it is Proust himself, her perverse lifelong accomplice, who is the fugitive, forever defying the power of language.

"On the off chance" or always by chance: the unpredictable and the contradictory, the paradoxical and the catch-22's, reign in place of the Other and its laws, preventing all chance of agreement and exchange. Proust will never be, like Kafka, a frighteningly punctual correspondent (who, in reality, saturates time with his punctuality and steals yours away). It takes luck (bad luck?) to run into Proust, the living roulette game—the gambler, snug in his cork-lined casino, who writes to others as he would bet on a number, in the hope that something unforeseen may happen. There is, moreover, a perfect consistency between his letters and his financial speculations (both conducted without guarantee or protection), since the latter are also conducted by mail. Proust's letters to his banker Lionel Hauser, more and more numerous over the years, are not insignificant. They show his absolute determination to thwart any kind of predictable contract. When Proust writes a letter, it is always more or less a gamble, more important in itself than for the possible profit he could make from it. Often he acts as if the potential gain had nothing to do with him, as if he is writing purely in order to lose, to *not* receive an answer. He exhausts the communicative powers of language, like his finances, with a strange pleasure. Both his letters and his financial dealings backfire through poor timing—sometimes missed by only a matter of hours. Timing is very important in his financial affairs, as with the Mexican streetcars that he sells too soon to make any money from them: "The Mexican tramway is running again, forty-eight hours too late. But, in the long run, trams are better off running—you just have to be careful not to miss the boat, or tram, as I did" (to Lionel Hauser, October 20 or 21, 1912).

Everyone knows that Proust, like Swann, dreams of train schedules. He dreams also of railway companies throughout the world and speculates on them at the stock exchange without the least prudence (again, everything is left to chance); and all is conducted through letters. From the "Light and Power" trams of Buenos Aires to those in Mexico, from the Southern Pacific to the Santa Fe railroad, from the North Caucasian to Suez, he travels and dreams, but of what? Of turning lead into gold? When the opposite actually happens and he loses time after time, even this is uncertain: "How has pure gold turned to worthless lead?" he asks (via Racine) L. Hauser (October 29, 1915). Could his speculations be just that? A means of traveling, of taking a train without leaving his room, without knowing his destination? A way of imagining that he has somewhere, at a distance, a gold mine of his own? "At the present moment my subtle mind, lulled by the waves, is sailing between the mines of Australia and the railways of Tanganyika and will alight on some goldmine which I hope will really deserve its name" (to Reynaldo Hahn, October 24, 1908).

Proust speculates on gold mines and streetcars—and on people. His maneuver to win back Alfred Agostinelli after their separation (echoed by Marcel's attempts at a reunion with Albertine) is revealing. He sends a telegram asking his friend A. Nahmias to offer a certain amount of money, anonymously and confidentially, to Alfred's father, with the suggestion that he persuade his son to return to Paris. He thus bets on Agostinelli Sr., in Monte Carlo, with the latter's son as the stake (though he must under no circumstances know about it):

> Make him understand that the person who sent you will know exactly whether or not the person in question has returned to Paris and stayed there and there is no chance for trickery, and that in order for the money to be sent regularly, the person must not only be back in Paris before the end of the week but must then not leave for a single day before April, and that if he tells him anything about this arrangement, the person who sends you will know immediately. And that he must on no account offer money to the person in question as that would make him behave in the opposite way and stay. *(to A. Nahmias, December 3, 1913)*

Everything is conducted secretly. Proust is a fan of the silent auction with sealed, mailed bids. Ideally, other people should know nothing about his personal gambles—for appearance' sake certainly, but there is also, in this extreme confidentiality, the desire that Agostinelli come back as if nothing has happened, as if by magic, as if Proust had won at roulette.

Agostinelli will never know about the financial exchange, and Proust too would prefer not to know about it. To quell the rumors (which will no doubt spread throughout France as soon as a telegram is sent) Proust refers to the affair as a *speculation:* "I warn you that by an extraordinary coincidence, the person who must not find out about our speculation is very well known where you are and, moreover, I am also well known to him, so send your telegrams yourself and, unless absolutely necessary, don't telephone because it's very difficult to hear & and that torments me but wire me often & soon" (to A. Nahmias, December 5, 1913). Later, when forced to cut back on his living expenses, he blames unlucky investments rather than expose the extent of the fortune he has spent on Agostinelli. In addition to the airplane he bought to keep Agostinelli amused, there are the countless sums Proust spends trying to recover his body from the sea near Antibes. To the bitter end, Proust spares no expense trying to bring back the one he desires, in order to eliminate his desire. It is as if he hopes for one last reassuring sign from Agostinelli's corpse—like Albertine's last letter telling Marcel she would like to come back to him, received after the telegram announcing her death.

Proust spends his life gambling on others and on their thoughts and desires. Instead of asking for something, he tries to win it. Speculation (which is, fundamentally, a work of the imagination) is Proust's favorite means of communication with others, while words and speech are repeatedly rejected or qualified. We can consider his letters a form of speech, but a very fragile one, inconsistent, often built on cliché and banalities, polite small talk incessantly repeated—empty, almost frozen words. Proust hides behind a protective glass wall, he makes gestures and follows conventions; his letters are simply calling cards, left at the door to excuse himself from an actual visit.[10] As for his real thoughts, he never verbalizes them, or if he does it is only in secret: the Other must not find out, no one must hear of it. Pretend I said nothing; the doctors forbid me to write anyway. Proust's correspondence is a long whisper, scattered with confidences and secrets— the last effort of an invalid swallowing his words, dead letters: "Hoping that this will stay between you and me and make *no noise*" (to E. Bibesco, June 28, 1907). His words are destined to consume themselves or to be retracted, sometimes both at once: "Burn this lettter, or rather send it back to me, as one can't burn letters in a house where there are no fires. I alone can do it!" (to Louis d'Albufera, July

8 or 9, 1908). His letters must come back to him to be burned. Bou-levard Haussmann is the most reliable language incineration center, and the only one that functions in July.

Mallarmé's Crayfish

"I am impersonal now: not the Stéphane you once knew" (to Henri Cazalis, May 14, 1867): Mallarmé's version of Rimbaud's "Je est un autre." To this staggering declaration, crucial for any self-respecting specialist, the late Mallarmé could have added: I am no longer within the realm of language (or at least unrefined language), I now only pretend to use it in my relations with the living, or with those who think they are alive, "so as not to be stoned by them, if they begin to suspect that they don't exist."[11] Mallarmé's "essential" and secret poetic language is a different matter. It concerns no one but him. Stéphane Mallarmé emerges from the crisis at Tournon with few illusions about communication. For more than thirty years he lives *beyond* the point of destruction of language with which Baudelaire, Proust, and Kafka were obsessed. In fact, he never comes back to it. What he wants is not a collapse of the symbolic, but its reduction to the lowest level, to the zero degree, where all social ties seem mere pretense. Mallarmé's work does not express the same obsessive defiance of the law as Kafka's or Proust's does; it illustrates instead a determined mourning of the Other. The "signifying convention" is a matter of pure convenience, and both his many occasional pieces and his letters illustrate this.

Mallarmé could have added one more statement to his note to Cazalis, his main confidant at the time: "I am no longer the letter writer I used to be." He writes it to others later, in a string of letters paradoxically as long as ever. To Jean Marras: "and we'll chat then, because it's too difficult to do in letters. I am no longer a letter writer at all" (January 2, 1886). Or to Jules Boissière who has sent him a densely written, six-page letter: "No, I cannot really answer your friendly chat which fills an entire evening with such charm! I, with my scraps of paper, have given up all forms of epistolary seduction" (November 24, 1892). Again to Octave Mirbeau: "I've given all letters up: for those we care about we write only through ourselves" (April 5, 1892). The announcement of his new "impersonality" also puts a check on his epistolary urges. His critics acknowledge this, in their own way, by rarely citing the letters written between 1867 and 1898 (the year in which the state officially confirmed Mallarmé's disappearance), and ignoring them with surprising confidence. It is as if there is, on the one hand, Mallarmé's correspondence (a thin volume most known for the famous letters from Tournon) and, on the other, as a footnote to his disappearance, a few hundred letters (almost ten volumes) considered insignificant, proof that the true correspondence ended earlier and that Mallarmé was no longer the letter writer he used to be. The more letters there are, the less important they seem. Nothing seems to happen there but seeming.

It is true that the letters dated after the crisis at Tournon can seem insignificant, marked by a weakness of some sort. But that is precisely what makes them symptomatic of something important. Their systematic blandness reveals, more than the earlier letters, the workings of one of the most lucid and unusual linguistic imaginations in existence. At the heart of this change is the fact that, as soon as he begins to construct his own poetic language, Mallarmé loses all involvement with his epistolary language. Rather, he uses letters to provide a solid contrast to his true work. His letters defy their own status as letters, they count for nothing. Their only goal is to be erased, like all the little notes he sends, scraps of conversations, scribbled out in pencil: "Farewell, dear friend. You'll read all this, written in pencil to give it the air of those good conversations between friends, away from the crowds with no raised voices." (to Paul Verlaine, November 16, 1885). Instead of a real correspondence (which would require a certain level of exchange and personal involvement), there are fragments of chitchat, pleasantries that never go beyond the surface and leave no lasting mark: "I'm saying all this as a form of conversation, as I'd like, moreover, to talk face to face with you. I'm at home to several friends, including you, on Tuesday evenings" (to René Ghil, March 7, 1885). Just a little chat or the expectation of a chat: there is nothing of substance in the correspondence; nothing requires an answer.

Mallarmé's letters arrange for small talk, and they *are* small talk. They are modeled on the famous "Tuesdays," Mallarmé's salon for young admirers on the rue de Rome, where the conversation is a kind of ritual, an art at which the Prince of Poets excels all the more for his lack of faith in the communication of personal experience. On the rue de Rome, the art of keeping one's distance replaces *savoir-vivre*. Mallarmé's letters limit his relations with others to a pure, often extremely polite gesture all the more charming because it represents a fundamental, sustained distance. His letters function as a simple salutation, a handshake, or a visiting card, sometimes all three at once: "Forgive me this visiting card, which represents a very warm handshake given in the midst of construction and moving!" (to A. C. Swinburne, May 10, 1876). They are like a coin that passes silently from palm to palm, far more subtle than humdrum words. The silence that the letters conceal is truly golden. The rest should not be written or spoken: "The only necessary letters, in my opinion, are business letters; because our real friends are those we can count on even in the most complete of silences, the silence we like to live and work in" (to Arthur O'Shaughnessy, July 14, 1877).

Mallarmé's correspondence becomes more and more formal as the years go by, as do the Tuesday rituals. The lack of critical importance attached to it at the time is at least partly due to his reticence and detachment. Mallarmé probably does this on purpose: by making his relationship with others a matter of *pure form*, he emphasizes the absence of a common linguistic measure in his poetics. Of all French writers, Mallarmé believes least in the possibility of an exchange through words. Yet through letters, he also makes the largest number of symbolic gestures—gestures that formally act out a relationship while leaving it empty of content, of all discursive expression that could engage the individual subject. Mallarmé's letters are a minimalist symbolic program, a means of handling the symbolic with no personal implications. They are the shadow of a word that has disappeared; Mallarmé lacks *presence* in his correspondence. It is an empty traffic of words and signs, a self-sufficient flow with no exterior purpose.

Mallarmé, in fact, often positions himself as the third party or intermediary between several of his correspondents. His correspondence is made to circulate, to multiply the formal ties between his different interlocutors. Between Banville and Payne, for example: "Banville talks about you every time I am able to see him" (to John Payne, July 3, 1872). Or between Verlaine and the Tuesday crowd: "I no longer see anyone, except on Tuesday evenings, my young friends; and you know that your name is mentioned there with the same enthusiasm by them as it is by me!" (December 8, 1884). Again, between Mirbeau and Geffroy, Monet, or Whistler (why stop at one?): "I don't think many days go by, my dear Mirbeau, without your name coming up in the discussions with Geffroy or Monet and others I meet . . . Just now I discussed you with Whistler and we spoke of seeing you again, and goodness me, since the day had been broken into I said: 'I'll write'" (April 5, 1892). Mallarmé's letters keep his correspondents informed of what others are saying about them. They form a kind of system or chain, as Mallarmé points out amusedly at the end of another letter: "You have thanked Manet for thanking you for sending your book; he thanks you in turn for having thanked him for thanking you; which forms a veritable chain which extends to your journey to Paris, each letter adding another link. You will reach the end of it" (to Arthur O'Shaughnessy, November 13, 1875).

Mallarmé becomes the catalyst and director of a confidential society of artists and writers, as he is during his Tuesday sessions and as he dreams of being for the reading rituals anticipated in the famous Book of which he speaks glowingly all his life. (See, in reference to this, Leo Bersani's pertinent analogy between the Tuesday salon and the Book.[12]) In 1873 he makes a genuine effort, with several friends, to organize an International Society of Poets. The organization's primary function would be to establish and maintain ties between people who are only "passing through." He speaks of the project in a letter to Frédéric Mistral: "My dear friend, what's involved is quite simply a form of free-masonry or guild. A certain number of us love something which is scorned: we ought to know how many we are, that's all, and we should know one another so that we can read each other, and visit each other when we travel" (November 1, 1873).

The idea is apparently soon dropped, but only in this form. Mallarmé's correspondence, as well as his other daily habits, demonstrate to what extent he remains a catalyst between others. He initiates young poets and allows others, already acknowledged members of the poetic community, to continue their participation in the group, even in their absence. The meetings are held as much through the mail as in person, and the poets travel through the letters they exchange. If the International Society of Poets exists only in letters, this is fully satisfactory for Mallarmé, perhaps better than any other option. The absent members provide topics of conversation for the people who do show up, and the meetings and letters become a chain of news and gossip binding them together. The most enjoyable discussions, however, are about dead members, whose absence from the ranks is all the more poignant and who will never spoil the conversation by offering their own opinions on themselves. While letters of mourning do not occupy much of Mallarmé's correspondence (though he does not skimp on condolences), all the letters after Tournon are structured like the *Tombeaux* he likes so much. Celebrations of the dead, commemorative passages, and attempts at communion with the absent are scattered discreetly throughout the letters, with Mallarmé as master of ceremonies. The most interesting result of death is that another person begins to speak in the place of the one who has died. Conversely, speaking about the dead person, speaking for him, requires one to die a little, to trade an "I" for a "he." One becomes, to some extent, another (or an Other). In order to change his identity, Mallarmé must either speak in the name of those who are absent—those who are neither "me" nor "you"—or be silent (though silence is always ambiguous). His letters combine the two possibilities. He is silent as much as possible with his elusive postal handshakes, and when he speaks it is about, for, or instead of others.

Mallarmé thus finds access to the impersonal through letters. At least Mallarmé's correspondence is one of the theaters in which the impersonal is played out—as it is in some of his occasional poems: not only the *Hommages* and *Tombeaux,* but also in undertakings like *La dernière mode*. Mallarmé edits the fashion magazine in order to disappear, hiding first behind the pseudonyms and the different aspects he takes on in the columns (all of which are written by him), and second behind his role as an intermediary between others. He controls the movements of his readers by suggesting places to go (sometimes even printing train schedules); he gives advice and keeps his readers au courant. He helps fads pass through at the right speed, ending them before they die, bringing in the new. He repeats what is being said and what one should be saying, and lists the new requirements of fashion. He repeats gossip and rumors, becoming part of that inattributable discourse belonging to no one in particular.

He also works, at approximately the same time, on the London magazine *Athenaeum,* writing a column called "Gossips" on the French literary and art worlds. The first time he writes about the column, he speaks of it as a letter from France:

> In the meantime, in order to create a tighter tie between the two literatures, couldn't we do something with the following idea? Would a letter on the literary movement sent from Paris regularly each week (a letter or notes) to be published in London in some interested magazine find

> a place and be of some use? I live in the perfect milieu to be aware of
> every important or interesting event here. *(to Richard Hengist Horne,
> March 10, 1875)*

His entire correspondence is organized on this principle of repetition
and circulation of news. He hides behind others' news, laying out
purely formal lines on absent people. The continuity between his
journalistic attempts and his letter writing is perfect. In letters like the
following one to O'Shaughnessy (cited above), Mallarmé's correspondence follows his plan for "Gossips" to the letter. (Again he has
an English correspondent—Mallarmé's Anglophilia allows him yet
another link in his chain and is perhaps inspired by the desire to extend his web across the Channel.)

> Here, dear Mr. O'Shaughnessy, are the few news items of the week; with
> the first showing of *Pompon,* an operetta which worries you as it does
> me, a buffoonery of Lecocq's, the musician of *Madame Angot;* it was
> not a success. The premiere also of a shameless melodrama by Belot,
> the author of various obscene and uninteresting novels, *La Vénus de
> Gordes,* that the critics have panned across the board and that the public
> is rushing to see before it disappears . . . But these things have been
> discussed so much in the French press that rumor of them has probably
> already reached London. I will write for myself somewhere a 'letter
> from Paris' in which I will take it as my duty to talk about even those
> things that are known; but not here, and I am sending only the few
> immediate items of literary or artistic interest that I hear discussed . . .
> All of this, to chat for a moment with you, before closing the envelope.

Where is Mallarmé? Buried beneath these greetings and gossips,
among the handshakes, pleasantries, and small talk. He is one of the
absent ones he repeatedly evokes. He is only a rumor.

Proust and Kafka use their letters to destroy language. They break it
down, making it say one thing and then the opposite, and sometimes
nothing at all. Mallarmé's letters on the other hand, lighten language;
they excuse it from its communicative duties, from all subjective

involvement and hidden meaning. They are as far away as possible from the confidential space that letters usually occupy. Mallarmé is a man without secrets, who tries desperately not to give the impression that he is hiding something, as this note to Manet's brother-in-law illustrates: "I'm attaching a note for Madame Manet to this letter, so that Edouard won't think we are corresponding behind his back and that we have something to say to each other, alas! that is hidden from him" (to Léon Leenhoff, April 6, 1883). Some try obstinately to conceal letters from the Other, to produce a confidential space. But Mallarmé does all he can to avoid even the appearance of corresponding behind someone's back. He writes to you so that another person will know of it, and you suddenly become the third party. Sometimes one has the impression that his only reason for writing is to prove that he has nothing to hide: he has nothing to say but he says it as publicly as possible, to allay all suspicion of a confidential relationship. Letters are replaced by the announcement of their existence. *Les loisirs de la poste* (Amusements of the Post) is a spectacular example of this—mailing addresses (made into quatrains) for insignificant notes intended for loved ones. They nearly replace the notes, as if the essential point is not the content of the letter but the declaration of its existence to the Other. (The Other is represented here by the mailman, who is the primary, necessary reader of these missives.) "This little publication, in honor of the Post Office. All of the addresses collated in verse here made it to their destination,"[13] begins a preface to these quatrains, in which Mallarmé insists on the privileged role of the mailman. *Les loisirs de la poste* acts out the ideal, emblematic chain that holds Mallarmé's correspondence together. It is also quite logical that the quatrains have been published with his letters by the editors of his correspondence.

Whether Mallarmé is functioning as an intermediary or requesting acknowledgment of his purely formal epistolary relationships, there is always a third party or "co-signer" involved—a mailman or an absent one to prevent any intimate speculation of the kind Proust liked so much. Mallarmé takes the confidential dimension out of letters by writing them for or with a third person. Intimacy in his life becomes a silence audible to everyone. Marie and Geneviève, Mallarmé's wife and daughter, are the most frequent co-signers of his letters, walking the narrow line between intimacy and the public domain: "I am leaving this greeting on your table. It is also from my daughter and her mother, who are with me." He almost always writes in the name of his family or instead of them: "My wife could tell you all of this for me. I don't know why I prefer to write to you: to give visible proof that I am alive" (to Théodore de Banville, November 1873). And he never forgets to inquire after the families of his correspondents; his letters are written primarily in order to send greetings to third parties. "Madame Mallarmé and Geneviève are going to catch up on your good mother's news and to talk endlessly with Mademoiselle Annette" (to François Coppée, July 22, 1872).

Over time Geneviève becomes a kind of secretary in the Mallarmé firm. She organizes her father's manuscripts and copies out his occasional poetry before it is dispatched (she is, after all, more reliable than the mailman). She sorts his mail and writes for him when he has arthritis or tired eyes: "It is I, Geneviève, who am writing, but it is papa who is speaking" (to Jean Marras, September 18, 1883); "I send, with my regrets, my apologies for using Mademoiselle, my secretary, to write to you" (to Berthe Morisot, December 11, 1886). Geneviève writes instead of her father who, for his part, never hesitates to take part in his daughter's correspondence: "I have committed the indiscretion of opening Madame's note to the ladies, who are not yet home, so as to answer it if it concerned this evening" (to Georges Rodenbach, October 1889). Madame Rodenbach sends a letter to Marie and Geneviève Mallarmé, and Mallarmé answers it in a note to Monsieur Rodenbach, just as he replies to the Gobillard sisters in Geneviève's name: "So, I am answering again, Demoiselles, because your Geneviève's hands are busy with other things. Your kind sympathy touches her, and if she manages to find some time when her patient doesn't need her, those few minutes of rest, at the front of the house, that she takes each afternoon, would be much brightened by your presence" (October 22, 1896). Geneviève looks after Madame Mallarmé, and Monsieur Mallarmé writes to her friends. The family is definitely close, too close for any privacy or secrets to exist. And that is what Mallarmé wants. If everything is openly discussed, there is nothing to explain and he need not answer any personal questions—he is untouchable. He puts his private life on display in order to avoid confiding in others about it and to avoid others' confidences. This perpetuates the lack of intersubjectivity that affords him his unique position as a writer. To gain access to the impersonal, Mallarmé turns himself into a universal father, a man without secrets, with nothing personal to tell and no life other than pure paternity.

There is only a small gap between pure and ideal fatherhood, and many of the Tuesday regulars on the rue de Rome manage to cross it. And who would make a more ideal father than Mallarmé? He is unfailingly kind and always responds nicely to the books and pamphlets he receives. He has no vices and no selfish desires. He never scolds and never asks for explanations. He is not like Hugo, who requires his disciples to imitate him. Nor is he one of those tyrannical fathers with their grotesque pleasures whom Kafka fears more than anything. Mallarmé is the perfect paternal role model, precisely because he wants to be a pure *referent*, an impersonal "he." His letters are fatherly and warm. He answers others without ever mentioning things that do not concern him. Unlike old Bendemann in Kafka's "Judgment," this father figure leaves you alone—he is too busy showing off the family he has really fathered.

Mallarmé's correspondence, then, creates a father-effect that is intimately connected to his impersonality. His main reason for writing letters is perhaps just that—to present himself to the world as an impersonal, generalized father. But his letters to Geneviève and Marie Mallarmé, written during the rare periods in which the family is sepa-

rated, are exactly the opposite. There is no longer a distant, simple
father-effect, but Mallarmé the real father strangely tormented by the
separation from his loved ones. The number of letters he writes increases accordingly. When he spends a few days alone at Valvins in his
country house, he sends daily detailed accounts of his life to Paris,
and receives copious and frequent replies. His family must be united,
everything discussed, and the same secrets shared. As soon as one
member of the family is missing, Mallarmé the letter writer becomes
frantic, as if even the least separation threatened the fatherly role that
constitutes his subjective space. It only takes a couple of days without
Geneviève (she is twenty-two and traveling for the first time without
her parents) for Mallarmé to lose his calm, to be overrun by the personal, almost Kafkaesque separation anxiety (to lose even his usual
serenity about the postal service):

> Our only worry (we don't worry over your absence, knowing that you
> are very happy) is about our correspondence. Letters and wires from
> here are cursed with bad luck—the other morning the mailman came
> by twice, yesterday your wire from 10:30 was in his hands until 4:30.
> So it may not have reached you before you left for Honfleur; and now,
> there you are, this morning, as I write this note which will follow you
> where? I don't know, with the delay of letters and the telegram. And I
> see that with these rapid movements, there is no time to pass on regular
> news. The most important is that you be informed about your mother;
> don't worry, she is not doing wonderfully, but is all right: I must have
> been very tactless on Sunday, which was one of her better days, to cause
> you so much anxiety. *(September 30, 1896)*

Mallarmé the subject? He is hidden in the anxiety inspired, for example, by his daughter's vacation. His constant denials and injunc-
tions not to worry convey his anxiety to Geneviève, and he will soon
call her home to care for her mother, whose health is not as good as
he pretends to believe. A separation from his family is almost the only
thing that will break Mallarmé's pattern of silent handshakes and reticent greetings: "I am answering your letter immediately, so that we

will be out of touch for the shortest time possible" (to Marie, September 23, 1875). At times he even becomes long-winded, as if the distance separating him from his loved ones will vanish if all is said—even, and especially, when there is nothing much to say. Mallarmé's country outings are not particularly eventful, but he describes them (mostly what he eats) at great length: "I don't want you to spend the whole day alone tomorrow, you will have at least my hello; too early perhaps, but you won't get it at all if I delay. I arrived by train, having eaten half a pâté from Doret's. For tonight, I have roast beef, for tomorrow night a ham; for lunch I will gobble up some eggs. With milk and asparagus to go with them, you see that I have no reason to complain" (to Marie, June 21, 1884). He tries to make Marie and Geneviève's mouths water, hoping to calm the worries he imagines them having: "Mother should not worry about anything. I will have to eat out three times this week (Madier, Seignobos, and Madame Laurent). The ham, the roast beef from the inn, some asparagus, shrimp, and strawberries, all cold, and—to warm me—soup and eggs, make up a perfectly satisfactory regime for the rest of the time" (June 3, 1885). Variations on gastronomy ward off anxiety.

Greed is the only sin that Mallarmé will admit to: "My only imprudence is to overeat lobster" (to Marie, September 13, 1873). Does he have other sins to confess? Are the lobsters and crayfish hiding other imprudences or excesses? There is his mistress, Madame Laurent, but she is just another crayfish: "The crayfish is you and that's enough for me" (to Méry Laurent, November 1895). She is part of the domestic-gastronomic sphere. She feeds Mallarmé in Valvins and receives letters like Geneviève's, written under the influence of seafood: "My little cat, I am writing under the influence of half a crayfish, bought in a basket on the rue des Martyrs to celebrate my last class of the year, to eat without mother having to cook, and to give me strength for the meeting of Julie Manet's guardians" (to Geneviève, July 26, 1892; he is Julie's tutor). And to Méry Laurent: "I won't write more, having eaten half a crayfish to give me strength for the upcoming meeting with the board of guardians" (July 26, 1892). Everyone knows about Méry Laurent anyway, and Mallarmé is not her only companion. No, the lobsters and crayfish hide nothing but Mallarmé's obsession with his paternal function, as the reference to Julie Manet shows. Mallarmé the father describes what he eats in order to give himself weight. *(Anatole, Anatole, pourquoi l'as-tu abandonné?)*

A Public Disturbance

His letters *are* literature, if you believe his editors: first Jacques Rivière, who opens the doors of the *Nouvelle revue française* to him by publishing the famous "Correspondance avec Jacques Rivière," then Henri Parisot, Paule Thévenin, and others, who never make any distinction between the letters and the literary texts. There is a continuity between the epistolary and the poetic in Antonin Artaud's work that his editors, like Rivière, cannot help seeing.

For some writers the act of writing is supported by a defiance of the law and by a destruction of the Other's credibility. Letters are one of the levers by which they trigger this destruction and give life to their ambiguous relationship to words. Artaud, however, resists this impulse—while strangely illuminating it. If his letters fall indisputably within the realm of literature and "poetic" writing, it is perhaps because of their constant struggle to reach an unreachable Other. They spring from the void left by a law that is always absent. Kafka, Proust, and Mallarmé write to escape the Other, defying it or reducing it to a matter of pure form. Artaud's Other, on the contrary, is elusive and unattainable, and this tactic is useless to him. (How can you dismiss someone you have never been able to apprehend?) Artaud writes almost in spite of himself, in a desperate and fruitless search for a guarantee or guarantor of his words. He would like to speak but cannot make himself heard by the Other, or by any other. His words escape him; they are only literature.

The "Correspondance avec Jacques Rivière" is a good example of this cycle. The facts are well known and unique. Rivière rejects some poems that Artaud sends him (they are generally not highly regarded today). Some time later he proposes the publication of the correspondence that followed the rejection, in which Artaud attempted to justify and explain his case to Rivière. Artaud accepts immediately, as if expecting the proposition: "For a long time I have been meaning to suggest to you that we put [the letters] together. I did not dare, and now your letter answers my desire. This is to tell you with what satisfaction I welcome the idea that you propose" (May 25, 1924). He enters the literary world through a substitution—of letters for poems—and an attempt at compensation: the correspondence with Rivière makes up for Artaud's lack of *address*, in all meanings of the word. Artaud compensates for his difficulty in expressing himself through his choice of correspondents, and Rivière steps in where the (poetic) language failed for lack of an audience or ideal reader. Up to this point, Artaud has been unable to imagine or desire a particular reader. His work has not been addressed to anyone and is thus condemned to perpetual disintegration: "I suffer from a horrible sickness of the mind. My thought abandons me at every level. From the simple fact of thought to the external fact of its materialization in words" (June 5, 1923).

This episode of Parisian literary life concludes happily, if one considers publication the desired end. In other ways, though, the affair seems to be based on a strange misunderstanding (noted by several critics).[14] Rivière sticks to his role as journal editor throughout the correspondence; he is a man of taste, an aesthete, compelled into the role of confidant by his duties at the *NRF:* "I shall always be delighted to see you, to chat with you, and to read anything you would like to submit to me" (June 23, 1923). He sees Artaud as a promising young man, a little overexcited but full of energy. He feels drawn to him and, toward the end of their correspondence, insists, against Artaud's will, on a relationship of identification: "You say that 'a man possesses himself in flashes, and even when he possesses himself, he does not reach himself completely.' This man is you; but I can tell you that it is also myself" (June 8, 1924). The identification in Rivière's last letter is all the more insistent for the fact that it is hopeless. He tries to maintain a position as confidant and literary adviser that Artaud denies him, convinced of the absolute singularity of his own case: "I resented your reply for a long time. I had presented myself to you as a mental case, a genuine psychic anomaly, and you answered me with a literary judgment on some poems which I did not value, which I could not value" (January 29, 1924). Even after the publication of the letters has been discussed, Artaud continues to emphasize his uniqueness: "The reader must believe in a real sickness and not in a phenomenon of the age, a sickness which touches the essence of the being and its central possibilities of expression, and which applies to a whole life" (May 25, 1924). The reader must believe that Artaud's illness is unique, and for this to happen, Rivière himself must also believe it. He must play the role of *guarantor* (or the Other).

Artaud has no interest in pleasant chitchat; he is not particularly talkative. The whole story begins when he *writes* to Rivière immediately after their first interview: "At the risk of imposing on you, I should like to ask you to reconsider a few points of our conversation this afternoon" (June 5, 1923). Rivière must answer for Artaud's words: "The question for me is nothing less than knowing whether or not I have the right to continue to think, in verse or in prose" (June 5, 1923). He becomes the final judge of Artaud's thoughts. This wish reappears throughout the correspondence, becoming more and more precise and urgent as time goes by: "To conclude, I am therefore sending you the latest product of my mind. In relation to myself it is worth little, although it is still better than nothing. It is a makeshift. But the question for me is whether it is better to write this than to write nothing at all. It is you who will give the answer by accepting or rejecting this little attempt" (January 29, 1924). The elusive Other is a dispossessing force. He steals Artaud's thoughts and takes words from the tip of his tongue. He removes Artaud from the realm of language; he is perceived as "Something furtive which robs me of the words *that I have found*, which reduces my mental tension, which is gradually destroying in its substance the body of my thought, which is even robbing me of the memory of those idioms with which one expresses oneself." (January 29, 1924). The words and the means of expression exist, or at least existed *before* he began to speak. As soon as he tries to express something, they disappear. The Other is, as Lacan claims, the location of the signifier, but a signifier that is inaccessible and unrealizable:

> to have within oneself the inseparable reality and the physical clarity of a feeling, to have it to such a degree that it is impossible for it not to be expressed, to have a wealth of words, of acquired turns of phrase capable of joining the dance, coming into play; and the moment the soul is preparing to organize its wealth, its discoveries, this revelation, at that unconscious moment when the thing is on the point of coming forth, a superior and evil will attacks the soul like a poison, attacks the mass consisting of word and image, attacks the mass of feeling, and leaves me panting as if at the very door of life. *(June 6, 1924)*

The Other as thief, stealing Artaud's speech: this motif, brilliantly analyzed by Jacques Derrida,[15] is at the heart of the correspondence with Rivière and is expressed there for the first time. Artaud has no interest in Rivière's friendship or his aesthetic judgment. He tries to force Rivière the individual into the position of the Other, guarantor of the truth and credibility of his words. He sees Rivière as a replacement for the inexorably unreachable Other, who empties language of its spoken potential and almost prevents him from existing, and looks to him to restore what is lost: "Restore to my mind the concentration of its forces, the cohesion that it lacks, the constancy of its tension, the consistency of its own substance. (And all this objectively is so little.) And tell me whether that which is missing in my poems (the old ones) could not be restored to them in a flash?" (January 29, 1924). Artaud's demonstrative second person is deliberately ambiguous, as if it is from Rivière that he really expects restitution. The transference effect here becomes part of his syntax, and Rivière is the exterior force that gives Artaud's words equilibrium, rhythm, and *credit*. "Trust me," "accept my reality," he asks several times. Again, when he refuses the "transposition" of the correspondence for publication: "The reader must believe in a real sickness." Rivière is called upon to prevent a collapse of the symbolic. If he gives Artaud credit, Artaud's words will be credible to everyone. If he so much as delays his response, Artaud immediately demands the return of everything entrusted to him: "My letter deserved at least a reply. Return, sir, letters and manuscripts" (March 22, 1924). Artaud does not want an analyst: as soon as Rivière falls silent, he enters the realm of Thief-Other.

But can Rivière break the silence? Is it possible for him to answer Artaud? In his last letter he writes: "I remain immobilized in the presence of sufferings which I can only dimly glimpse. But perhaps this attitude of bewilderment will provide you with more help and encouragement than my previous ratiocinations" (June 8, 1924). How can he answer someone who denies him his own speech and demands something that is strictly intransitive, who wants neither a friend nor a listener but someone who will take him literally? It is worth noting that when Artaud explicitly claims his "right" to write, the second person often disappears from his language: he is addressing no one—or everyone except Rivière, the partner in the dialogue. Rivière's replies are off the mark. Worse, he does not recognize the absolute singularity of Artaud's case and he tries to the bitter end to understand, advise, and identify with him. In return, he is dismissed as a person, expected to disappear, no more no less. Later (as Laurent Jenny has noted), Artaud comments: "It has always seemed very strange to me that he died so soon after having published these letters."[16] It is as if Rivière had actually disappeared because of the exchange and its publication.

Rivière's blindness to the strange transference inflicted on him is easy to understand. (Although he is surprised by the mastery of expression in Artaud's letters, he never thinks about the role he plays in their production.) It is equally easy to understand his reluctance to publish Artaud, to step down from his privileged position and become a simple witness or instrument allowing Artaud, who has never really been his partner in dialogue, to enter into an exclusive relationship with the Other. Rivière resists the invisibility Artaud tries to inflict on him until the very end of their correspondence, even when proposing the publication of the letters: "An idea has occurred to me which I have resisted for some time but which I find extremely attractive" (May 24, 1924).

By publishing the letters, Rivière relinquished the role of intimate confidant and ideal reader that he played for Proust and so many others. He allowed the letters to become what they always were for Artaud: addressed not to a person but for publication. Artaud's immediate and positive reaction to Rivière's proposal leaves little doubt on this point. In his mind, the letters replace the poems (whose failure he fully acknowledges) and are written, as the poems were, in order to be published. Rivière is simply an intermediary between Artaud and an invisible Other, who for once will be unable to remain silent and ignorant. He will no longer be able to steal Artaud's words from him, furtively opening his letters before they are sent. The letters are now public. They are an act of protest, Artaud's way of making noise, refusing to give in. Ireland is not the only site of his public disturbance (he is hospitalized from 1937 on). All of his writing—his correspondence in particular—may be seen as a form of public disturbance of the peace.

Open letters, protests, and provocations: the correspondence with Rivière is only the beginning. This tactic later provides Artaud's common ground with the surrealists, before he is ostracized for his extremism. We know that André Breton found him frenetic, too prone to take things to heart or to take them literally. What if he acted on his impulses, went out in the street with a revolver and fired on the crowd? To bring the surrealist metaphor into reality would destroy it and would send Artaud to an insane asylum all the sooner. (This is exactly what Artaud seemed to want.) His correspondence with Rivière foreshadows the great letters from Rodez twenty years later, the main difference being that Artaud no longer fixes his discourse on any one person. Without Rivière, he is cast adrift. Where before he had the perfect guarantor of his subjectivity, he now has only the wandering flow of letters, written to denounce the Other (all others who represent the law that has crushed him). He writes to protest his dispossession, the tricks and intrigues organized to silence him and make him disappear:

> There is an old matter which everyone is talking about privately but which no one in ordinary life is willing to talk about publicly, although it is happening publicly all the time in ordinary life, something which, through a kind of nauseating mass hypocrisy, no one is willing to admit that he has noticed, that he has seen and experienced. This matter is a kind of mass spell-casting in which the whole world more or less participates off and on, while pretending not to be aware of it, and trying to hide from themselves the fact that they participate in it, now with their unconscious, now with their subconscious, and more and more with their full consciousness. The purpose of this spell-casting is to prevent a plan of action which I undertook years ago, which is to get out of this stinking world and to have done with this stinking world. *(to Henri Parisot, September 17, 1945)*

Artaud's madness now falls into the public domain: everyone knows about it but it is never discussed. No one gives him credit or acknowledges his dispossession. He cannot even claim it publicly, as he did with Rivière. The Other is a thief who never gets caught because everyone has conspired to let the robbery happen. Artaud writes an ever-increasing number of letters, to break the silence and to shed new light on old news, to publicize what everyone already knows.

With Rivière he had some security, a guarantor. From Rodez he addresses his letters exclusively and systematically *against* the Other. Like all of Artaud's correspondents at this point, Parisot is simply a substitute for Rivière. He is an instrument for Artaud's public denunciations, charged with the publication of the letters he receives: "I ask you to publish this letter, which André Breton would certainly have been delighted to publish twenty-five years ago in *La Révolution surréaliste*" (September 22, 1945). Each letter becomes implicitly (sometimes explicitly) a corrected proof, ready for publication, and its addressee is an accomplice whose understanding is unspoken. Or he is at least supposed to be. In the end, despite Artaud's attempts to increase the number and variety of the letters he sends, he receives in return only silence and neglect. The spell always wins out. The correspondent passes from tacit complicity to enemy lines. Artaud is constantly forced to remind his correspondents what they should already know, what their infidelity and insincerity make them forget. Thus, barely two weeks after the September 22 letter, Artaud writes to Parisot again, this time to denounce and accuse him: "I assure you, dear Mr. Parisot, that I am not pleased with you and that I am even terribly furious with you. I told you a dark story which you refused to believe, not because it was unbelievable, but because you placed a spell on yourself so as not to believe it, and I accuse you of having done this knowingly and consciously at a certain time on a certain day, preferring to believe that life continues" (October 5, 1945). Soon afterward, Artaud (very provisionally) withdraws his permission for the publication of the *Voyage au pays des Tarahumaras*, Parisot's original reason for writing to him.

The recipients of the Rodez letters are in just as impossible a position as Rivière was earlier, though for opposite reasons. Rivière was a prerequisite for Artaud's self-expression; Parisot and the others are a hindrance. Artaud resents having to write to them, and they are condemned to walk his imperceptible line between the hostile outside world and an understanding where words are superfluous. The ambiguity and the extraordinary tension of the Rodez letters comes from the fact that they are intended to function beyond language; they are a constant attack on words. Artaud's correspondents should understand him without the help of words. If they need language, it is because they are blinded by the spell of the Other. They are merely pretending not to know or understand. The letters are written to explain this and to expose his correspondents' blatant infidelity, their subjection to language. Artaud's words are always backed by a rage against the language that serves him only as a means of denouncing its users.

As for Artaud, he is no longer a part of this language. Or perhaps he has just lost all desire to be. He tries instead to make up his own language—just as he untiringly reinvents his past. The fact that there is, in the Rodez letters, an attempt on Artaud's part to recreate himself, superimposed on the gesture of denunciation of the Other, is understandable. He tries to return to the original moment of his dispossession, recounting his story over and over. He racks up countless variations, a last effort to reverse the movement and to force back the Other: he has been stabbed in Marseille by a bewitched pimp, he was the victim of a plot in Afghanistan, of voodoo and orgies in Paris, he has seen opium fields burned or trafficked by the English in China— stories that go "back to before the flood and well before the creation" (to Henri Parisot, October 9, 1945). He extends his story to the beginning of time. He invents a new genealogy for himself, an origin that preceded the Other, preceded all sexuality (the filth evoked in his abundant variations on "I am my father, my mother, my son and myself") and, perhaps more important, preceded language. No reinvention of the self is possible without a reinvention of language—and this is the motivation behind his infamous "glossolalia," Artaud's form of speaking in tongues: *"ortura ortura konara kokona kokona koma"* (to Parisot, September 22, 1945). He goes back to the moment at which language became a threatening and hostile force in order to recreate himself as a subject:

> For years I have had an idea of the consumption, the internal consummation of language by the unearthing of all manner of torpid and filthy

necessities. And in 1934 I wrote a whole book with this intention in a language which was not French but which everyone in the world could read, no matter what their nationality. Unfortunately, this book has been lost. It was printed in a very limited edition, but abominable influences on the part of people in the government, the church, or the police caused it to disappear. *(to Henri Parisot, September 22, 1945)*

A universal language, transparent and comprehensible to everyone, is no one's language (and no Other's language). But again it falls prey to one of the Other's nasty tricks; he steals the new language invented to destroy him. Artaud's other language and the book that contained it now exist only in a radically separate space. And the complete book—an idea Mallarmé also had but did not pursue—will never exist.

All that is left of Artaud's supreme language are the glossolalia. Mere "attempts at language," syllables, linguistic experiments, the leftovers or by-products of his Book:

> Here are a few attempts at language which must be similar to the language of that old book. But they can only be read rhythmically, in a tempo which the reader himself must find in order to understand and to think: *ratara ratara ratara* . . . but this is worthless unless it gushes out all at once; pieced together one syllable at a time, it no longer has any value, written here it says nothing and is nothing but ash; to bring it to life in written form requires another element which is in the book that has been lost. *(September 22, 1945)*

Debris of a universal language, the glossolalia are a pale imitation of once powerful speech, fallen into writing. They have neither the breath nor the rhythm needed to communicate. They are the meager ghosts of an outburst captured alive in the book. They are the incandescent margins where the book destroyed itself, becoming open letters and public announcements. They pierce the Rodez letters with their devastating universality. In the glossolalia, a unique language becomes an epistolary gesture addressed to and against everyone. They appear in some letters and not in others, surfacing as if by chance or following the rhythm of Artaud's anger. They are unforeseeable and have no relation to the meaning or subject of the letters. They are simply the extreme manifestation of a syntax that has worn itself out by not making sense and has no foundation left. They mark the failure of language to transmit a subject. In this way, present or absent, the glossolalia form the core and fundamental punctuation of the Rodez letters, the moorings from which all the intersubjective cables cast off.

chapter three

Images, Memories, Mourning

All the writers discussed in this book practice some form of epistolary perversity. Their letters reinforce distances. They preempt the possibility of exchange or agreement. Addressed by necessity to an absent other, the letters not only deny their readers any subjective individuality but also work toward their total disappearance. The absence of an addressee allows the letters to exist and justifies their existence; it is also their goal or cause. At the heart of the epistolary mode, there is the need to destroy relationships—a mental attempt to dissolve what is solid, to replace a correspondent with his shadow, or to bury him beneath the image one has of him.

The destructive gesture turns, paradoxically, into a creative one. The absent correspondent must be replaced by an image or representation. "I think of you often" is a commonplace of letters. But it can also mean much more. For some writers, the act of imagining the other takes priority over all else and becomes the goal of the correspondence. Instead of building a relationship with the real person, the letter writer imagines her, creates her, thinks about her, and then writes to tell her so. Proust, for example, seems to write to others solely to inform them that he is thinking of them; or, perhaps more important, he seems to think of them solely so that he can write to them.

He spends days imagining what the company of his correspondents would be like and lives with them in his mind. This is the most constant motif in Proust's correspondence and is discussed directly many times in the letters: "The thought of you keeps me such delicious company every day that to receive a letter from the person who hasn't left my mind seems to me at once completely natural and almost miraculous" (to Madame Straus, April 24, 1910). Thinking of Madame Straus and others every day is the activity that sustains our apprentice writer's epistolary compositions. For Proust letter writing becomes a kind of professional moonlighting, more time-consuming than it appears when one considers the number of people he knew. He spends so much time imagining his correspondents that he has no time to see them; this in turn allows him to think of them even more, even obliges him to do so: "Thank you for your letter; time hangs heavy on me without having seen you again and I miss you all very much. I've thought of you *every day*. But don't come; I'm too disorganized to 'receive'" (to Madame Léon Fould, around March 15, 1908).

The phrase "I think of you" begins as a cliché of epistolary rhetoric. But, after much use and abuse, it becomes the foundation of Proust's letters. He passes from "I'm writing because I'm thinking of you" to "I'm writing *in order* to think of you." (Here we must understand as well, inseparable from the second statement, "I think of you in order to write to you." Writing to and thinking of others are always two sides of the same coin.) And his correspondence grows out of this literal translation of a cliché.

He thinks of his loved ones and acquaintances constantly and never fails to inform them of his thoughts in writing. Having begun a letter, he thinks of them all the more, and more interestingly: "You know I always think of you when I am writing. Besides, I constantly think of you even without that, but all the more when I am more myself and more worth-while, consequently most of all when I write" (to Georges de Lauris, March 24, 1912). An ongoing correspondence requires one to think of others, to speculate about them in their absence. Proust thus uses his correspondents to people the separate and singular space he has built through letters. His space becomes not only livable but lived in, and these imaginary others give meaning and charm to his epistolary isolation. The activities of his imagination are all the more appealing for the fact that nothing real interferes with them. His "I think of you every day," is also a "You seduce me every day," maintained through a string of letters and the distance they produce. The marquise is incredibly beautiful, at this distance: "I am, alas, not at all sure to be able to go to see Madame Lemaire on Tuesday. Though the temptation of being presented to you at last is great! I spend my time 'imagining' you by gathering together all the beautiful things different people say. Combined, they make 'you,' as I know you! But it would not be disagreeable to confront this abstraction with the reality" (to the Marquise de Casa Fuerte, June 5, 1910). Proust versus Valéry: It would be a pleasure to be introduced to the marquise, but he would have to leave by five o'clock. In the meantime it is not disagreeable to imagine her, and perhaps even better this way: he can dream of her as the chambermaid to the Baronness Putbus, and even write a novel about it. Time spent thinking of others and about others, instead of seeing them or talking to them, is not necessarily wasted. And it is definitely better for his health. He is sometimes so carried away by his thoughts of others that he forgets his illness: "I am writing to you with a high fever and it requires the attraction of the correspondent I imagine while writing for me to overcome it and write to you" (to Charles d'Alton, October 29, 1910). To live happily, live in your imagination. Letters have a therapeutic value that Proust will find again only in the composition of his great novel.

The Image Hunters

Each writer uses letters to build up a store of images. Proust evokes all others—or at least all of the beau monde—and paints imaginary portraits of them, raw material for future novels. Other writers focus, photographically, on one subject. Flaubert feels as strongly about the images and memories he has of Louise Colet as he does about Louise herself. It is as if he pursues his relationship with her in order to remember it later, and to remember himself as he was when with her, as he no longer is when he writes to her. Where now *is*, his letters make what *was* appear. They fix, mount, and frame it like a picture. This tendency appears in the very first words written to Louise: "Twelve hours ago we were still together, and at this very moment yesterday I was holding you in my arms! Do you remember? How long ago it seems!" (August 4–5, 1846). The passage from first-time lover to Orpheus took less than twelve hours.

Everything begins—and ends—with the first meeting. It becomes inexorably part of the past, to be revived in Flaubert's letters for days and weeks: "Twenty times a day, I see you again, with the dresses I know on you, the expressions I've seen. I undress you and redress you in turn" (August 24, 1846). Flaubert undresses Louise in memory and by mail. His sentimental education is an exercise in recall. The moon always shone yesterday.

> The sky is clear, the moon is shining. I hear sailors singing as they raise anchor, preparing to leave with the oncoming tide . . . Moths are playing around my candles, and the scent of the night comes to me through my open windows. And you, are you asleep? Or at your window? Are you thinking of the one who thinks of you? Are you dreaming? What is the color of your dream? A week ago we were taking our beautiful drive in the Bois de Boulogne. What an abyss since that day! For others, those charming hours doubtless went by like those that preceded them and those that followed; but for us it was a radiant moment whose glow will always brighten our hearts. It was beautiful in its joy and tenderness, was it not, poor soul? *(August 8–9, 1846)*

Flaubert's letters are structured like memories. More precisely, they try to pin memories down so that they can be read and transmitted. "Are you thinking of the one who thinks of you?": literally, are you remembering the same instant as I am? Sharing the same image in thought, letting that "radiant moment" light up the same two hearts, whose meetings are now so brief, buried in obscurity? When all is said and done, memories are perhaps the happiest time they ever had.

Reminiscences about first meetings are a commonplace in romantic relationships. But there is, in Flaubert's insistence on his first meeting with Louise, something that goes beyond the simple cliché. Expressed with such intensity, it takes on a strangely real weight. (Flaubert is one of many writers who manage to revitalize the rhetorical cliché they have been tricked into believing.) He collects images the way other people collect keepsakes. He stores his letters from Louise alongside the treasured objects she has given him, which he refers to repeatedly, almost ritually (he has, after all, a simple heart): "When evening comes and I am alone, certain not to be disturbed, and around me everyone is asleep, I open the chest of drawers I told you about and I pull out my relics, spreading them out on my table, the little slippers first, the handkerchief, your lock of hair, the bag with your letters, I reread them, I touch them again" (August 23, 1846). He surrounds himself with the keepsakes he sends and receives, letters of recollection and of commemoration.

Flaubert's letters to Louise always involve an act of memory—performed by Louise as well as Flaubert, since his images of her always have her lost in thought, remembering something or writing about it. Through these dreams of Louise, Flaubert is able to remember himself and celebrate the man that he was: "I dream about your pose as you write to me, the long looks you throw as you turn the pages over. It is under the lamp which lent its light to our first kisses, on that table where you write your poems. In the evening, light your alabaster lamp, look at its white, pale light while remembering the evening we loved each other" (August 23, 1846). His letter authenticates the memory, fixing it permanently in the room where everything happened for the first time. The pristine scene in the light of an alabaster lamp becomes a scene of writing. The Louise whom Flaubert held in his arms metamorphoses into a Louise who is writing to him, thinking of him in the poses he imagines, and staring into the void his departure has left behind. The letters follow a closed circuit of images conveying absence.

Flaubert's letters are made up of fragments of visual scenes, imagined or remembered in silence. He writes less to make himself heard than to make himself seen. "Do I like you! Do I love you! A deaf man who saw me writing to you would know the answer: he would only have to *look* at my body" (August 26, 1846). Does he love her? The blind are not sure, but the deaf know it well. Perhaps only the deaf would believe it, since no declaration of love leaves Flaubert's mouth without a qualification that destroys its magic and its integrity. Louise repeatedly demands a verbal description of his love, and he stubbornly answers her only with the inspirations of a lover wholly fulfilled by letters and images: "You cannot see my smiles when I receive your letters, or the joy that must be on my face when I think of you or look at your portrait, the portrait with its long, caressing locks that have fallen onto my cheeks and that my lips have nibbled" (August 31, 1846). If only Louise could be satisfied with the portrait Flaubert paints of himself as a bashful lover, surrounded by letters and mementos. If only she were more like him—the great *rêveur*, sleepily satisfied with the thoughts of his mistress: "Twenty-four hours ago: remember! Oh, the impossibility of recapturing any part of a thing that is gone! Adieu, I am going to bed now, and before sleeping I'll read there the letter you wrote me while waiting for me" (August 20–21, 1846). "I rest in the memory of you as on a comfortable bed. I give myself over to you, I breathe you in" (October 8, 1846).

If only Louise were content with the way he consumes and assimilates her by mail. Instead she blindly ignores the fact that her liaison with Flaubert is an affair of images and that the relationship has never been more than a series of poses and looks, carefully remembered and preserved in letter after letter. She does not even remember their first meeting, for example, despite Flaubert's constant reminders (it is his favorite image). She was posing for Pradier the sculptor, in his studio, when Flaubert was introduced to her. Already his primary image of her was visual:

But do you know the two pictures of you that predominate? In the studio, standing, posing, the light falling on you from the side, when I was looking at you and you at me. And then the night at the hotel—I see you lying on my bed, your hair streaming over my pillow, your eyes raised, your face pale, your hands joined, flooding me with wild words . . . And I? Tell me how I seem to you, what sort of picture of me comes to your mind? *(August 13, 1846)*

It is not surprising that he always prefers to see her in painting. All of Flaubert's letters describe his passion for images, at least all of them when he gets passionate about anything. His apathy gradually increases and the pursuit of images, so important during the first weeks of the correspondence, becomes more discreet in time. It does not reappear during the reprise of the relationship in 1851. The affair trails off—perhaps in line with Flaubert's capacity for imagery. His ability to see himself as a figure from the past slowly disappears.

The meeting at the Brods' in August 1912 is a kind of visual echo to the one in Pradier's studio. Before even mentioning Palestine, Kafka shows Felice the photographs of his recent trip to Weimar (where he initiated Elisabeth Kirchner into the pleasures of letter writing). He is not really a traveler and he will be a mediocre lover and fiancé, but he is, without question, a specialist of images.

Images overpower everything that follows in Kafka's letters to Felice. No other epistolary exchange illustrates a stronger determination to create and sustain them. In the early days of the correspondence (before their actual meetings disturb the pattern), Kafka's desire to *see* Felice is unremitting. When he runs low on visual images, the entire correspondence is threatened: "I'm afraid that soon I shall no longer be able to write to you, for to be able to write to someone . . . one has to have an idea of the face one is addressing" (November 14, 1912). His letters to Felice (with her insignificant looks) attempt to piece together an idea of her and to sustain an image that will in turn sustain the writing. But this is impossible without some input from her—she must furnish the raw material for Kafka's imagination to build on. She barely manages to answer one letter from Kafka when he starts to bombard her with questions:

> On the other hand, what good does it do me to learn about your visits to the theater if I don't know everything that happened before and after, if I don't know what you wore, which day of the week it was, what the weather was like, whether you dined before or after, where you sat, in what kind of mood you were and why, and so on, as far as thought can reach. Of course it is impossible to tell me everything, but then everything is impossible. *(October 24, 1912)*

No one can do the impossible except, apparently, Felice. The fact that there is always something missing in her letters does not excuse her from writing. On the contrary, she must write more and more to fill in the gaps in the information she has already provided. When it comes down to it, the fundamental thing missing in all the letters carried from Berlin to Prague is the image of Kafka himself, and that empty space is perhaps just what he wants to see. He studies the descriptions of Felice's life and the photographs he begs her to send, looking for his own absence; he literally de-picts himself. We are very far here from the pleasures of the visual: Kafka is not interested in his own reflection, but in the reflection of scenes that exclude him. His desire for images of Felice is matched only by his reluctance to be seen by her or to send his own photograph.

The images Kafka solicits (and receives) prove above all that he plays no role in the pictures Felice paints of her life. He is present only as a ghostly third party, an invisible man. When Felice goes to the theater, he imagines her through others' eyes, almost as if she herself is the dancer the audience has come to watch. The scenes that elicit the greatest number of comments and questions are generally tied to these public moments in Felice's life. In his favorite images of her, she is always in the presence of others who are looking at her, others he can never join. He tangos with her in Berlin by proxy:

Oh, what a good time you are having, I can see you dancing with the chief clerk Salomon, then with the gentleman who writes poetry, then with all 6 gentlemen who were around your desk yesterday when you wrote to me . . . You make me quite giddy with all your dancing. And undoubtedly they all dance better than I do. Ah, if you could see me dance! You would throw up your arms! But please go on dancing, I am going to sleep, and to spite them all with the power of dreams, God willing, I shall draw you, dearest, out of the throng of dancers calmly to my side. *(December 1, 1912)*

Kafka corresponds with Felice in order to create an image of her but also, like Flaubert (and even more radically so), to contemplate his absence from the image, to confirm his existence in a "non-place"—where he will never be recognized because he will never be seen. Instead of a portrait of himself, Kafka sends Felice a photograph of a cloud: "Should someone ask you what your fiancé looks like, say you have taken a photograph and show them the enclosed little cloud. It really is me, and you actually took the photograph" (May 24, 1914).[1] He imagines himself near her, invisible, in the blue of the sky. His distant speculations on Felice's outings place him again in an unshareable space, which finds its double in Felice's bedroom: "I still know so little about your room, dearest, and when in my thoughts I try to follow you there I am lost and somewhat in the dark" (December 1, 1912). He cannot imagine himself there and remains somewhat in the dark, not so much because Felice has never described the room as because she will never be able to describe his absence from it, the intrusive void that he occupies there.

The equivalent strength of Kafka's passion for letters and photographs is fully understandable. He sees himself in every photograph that he demands, scrutinizes, and analyzes. Absent or invisible, he is the lens that captures and possesses Felice: "Oh, dearest, what nostalgic pleasure these pictures give! They all represent my dearest one; each is different from the others, they all take hold of one by force . . . You sit there so quietly, your left hand completely idle, yet it cannot be seized, something requiring thought is being dictated. An ingenious photograph in the event of one having planned to kiss the mouth" (January 12–13, 1913). As such, Kafka provides a frame for each image. He trims the photographs sent to him, enlarging the smallest details, without ever losing sight of what is missing from the image (hence his extreme sensitivity to what the position of the camera has cut from the scene itself): "What a beautiful, delicately worked dress you are wearing in the picture, and what is the rest of it like? Are you standing, or sitting? Your right arm is missing. That shiny thing, is it the locket?" (January 26, 1913).

All of Kafka's letters seem geared toward the description of beautiful images and, inversely, all the photographs he likes seem to be taken for the epistolary commentary they inspire. There is a profound continuity between these two practices. A photograph is like a concentrated letter, the essence of writing distilled. It keeps your attention, you can't put it down. It keeps you company when you travel, turning tedious business trips into pleasure trips. It will even accompany you to your hotel room.[2] "During the whole trip your photograph was looked at now and then for comfort, and for comfort your photograph spent the night on a chair beside my bed" (November 26, 1912). There are the photographs you place beside your bed and those you take to bed with you: "And in bed, with your photograph, what a lovely way to spend one's time! Unhappiness could not touch me; it had to wait at my bedside; as long as I stayed in bed, I was completely protected" (December 15, 1912).

The letter writer takes refuge from the world. His letters build a protective wall around him. And inside the wall he has photographs—the images he has demanded of the other—to calm and entertain him. Only photographs can halt the flow of Kafka's letters: "But I am so engrossed in the picture I don't get a chance to continue this letter—something you never considered, dearest, when giving the present" (December 26–27, 1912). "I am so engrossed in the picture" is even more compact in German: *so verschaue ich mich*. A "sich verschauen," a loss of oneself in the image one is looking at, a *de-piction*: the final goal of Kafka's correspondence and its traffic of images.

Telepathy

In the letters of Kafka, Flaubert, and Proust, images are always projected onto a distant horizon. They emerge where the letter disappears. There is, in the writers' epistolary passion, a secret desire to be rid of letters, to create a space in which they are unnecessary, where thoughts and images are conveyed wordlessly, magically, and immediately as easily and simply as light captured by the eye or the camera lens.

Letters are often exhausting. You write, you argue, you reason, sometimes—as in Kafka's case—to the point of discouragement and disillusionment. The letter writer becomes increasingly frustrated by his inability to enter the stream of images he creates or to enjoy the kind of automatic transmission of thought and sight that his letters can only imitate. And as he tries to rid himself of words, to cut himself off from language, he writes all the more desperately and voluminously. He longs to disappear into an image, to become an image, but language clings to him like a second skin. Shed only briefly, it grows again, bringing distance and separation with it. He cannot use language to escape language.

This is why nothing pleases our writer more than coincidences and unspoken agreements. Nothing fascinates him more than the moment when his thoughts are perfectly synchronized with those of his correspondent, defying the distance between them. Kafka's letters are most successful when they become unnecessary, when they are overtaken by events. And his happiness is the greatest when the telepathy centers on images. He is elated, for example, when he receives—without asking—a portrait of Felice, which he then carries with him everywhere. He is even more ecstatic when Felice requests a photograph of him just after he has sent her one: "Again we have been of one mind. In your last letter you remind me of my photograph; I got that letter probably the very moment you received mine, written yesterday, with the picture in it. But there is also something unfulfilled. Both letters say we want to meet, but it does not happen" (November 29, 1912). What could be better, for the inveterate letter writer, than to receive an unsolicited image, against a backdrop of impossible reunion?

Through letters Kafka tries to evoke the images and thoughts that can replace letters, bypass them, leave them behind like spirits escaping the body. For the distance and space created by the original discord of an unrepeatable meeting, Kafka substitutes a kind of "outer space" where thoughts drift weightlessly, silently, with no resistance— as if he were on the moon, or farther still. He dreams of turning letters into dreams; he longs for everything to be effortless, for desires to be fulfilled before they have even been formulated. The impossible goal of the correspondence is not so much to write the perfect love letter as to experience the love before the letter describes it:

> Dearest, have you noticed how astonishingly of one mind we are in our letters? If there is a question in one, the following morning brings the answer. The other day, for instance, when you wanted me to say I love you, I had felt compelled to put the answer in the letter that crossed yours that night somewhere between here and Berlin; but perhaps it was obvious anyway from the opening words of my very first letter, or even from the first casual look I gave you that evening. There have been so many examples of our mutual understanding that I have lost count. *(November 24, 1912)*

Everything has already been said in the first words of their first letter—or even earlier, in the first look they exchanged, no doubt unnoticed at the time. The letters are born of that first look whose "message" they repeat endlessly, and they are also limited by it. They try repeatedly to return to it, disappear into it, revive it with images.

Through letters the insignificant face, originally looked at with such indifference, becomes a captivating, irresistible sight.

The letter writer dreams of being a dreamer. Kafka, as Pierre Pachet has noted, is strangely attracted to sleep.[3] An insomniac, he hopes to find in letters what others find in dreams: it is almost as if his letters allow him to watch himself dream. Instead of sleeping beside Felice, he puts her to sleep time after time. He delights in imaginary depictions of scenes he denies himself access to in reality. (Without prohibitions or taboos, according to Freud, we would have nothing to dream about.) For Kafka letters replace sleep (how many nights he spends writing to Felice, and how little time he has left to sleep!). His letters are intended to be a flow of surprising thoughts and images, a reproduction of the dream or hypnotic state.

Kafkaesque letter writing is a kind of sleepwalk *à deux*. He writes, standing (or sitting) in a waking dream, and she sleeps: "You must have been asleep for sometime, and it is unfair of me to jeopardize your sleep with this little postscript" (November 3, 1912). When he imagines his letters' arrival at Felice's house, he sees her resting, his thoughts conveyed to her like a foreign language absorbed in her sleep. He takes an almost fanatical interest in her nocturnal habits. He stays awake in order to speak to her while she sleeps. And she is required to sleep all the more because he gives up his sleep to watch over her. He entrusts his epistolary insomnia to her unconscious mind, placing his waking thoughts beneath her closed eyelids. He tries to come to her as a dream:

> Are you asleep? Or are you still reading—of which I would disapprove? Or are you still at a rehearsal? I most sincerely hope not. By my watch, always slow but never out of order, it is now 7 minutes to 1. Remember, you should sleep more than other people, for I sleep less, though not much less, than most. And I can't think of a better place to store my unused share of universal sleep than in your beloved eyes. And no wild dreams, please! In my mind I am making a tour around your bed, de-

manding silence. And after I have put everything in order there, and perhaps even shooed away a drunk from the Immanuelkirchstrasse, I return, more orderly within myself as well, to my writing, or perhaps even straight to sleep. *(November 14, 1912)*

He is the jealous watchman of Felice's rest, demanding silence and chasing away everything that could disturb her. She must sleep peacefully and dreamlessly, while his words take the place of what she would dream if he did not write. This is undoubtedly the root of his obsession with his fiancée's rest: since he can communicate with her only through dreams, she will never sleep long enough to please him.

Flaubert feels a similar tenderness when his thoughts and feelings are fully synchronized with Louise's, like a photographic image developing simultaneously in Croisset and Paris—above and beyond the endless letters they write in which nothing ever coincides and which serve only to multiply the misunderstandings and reproaches. To counteract the letters' friction, Flaubert and Louise must, from time to time, abandon them and simply *see* the same things at the same time. Too much writing in the dark ruins their vision; in writing, they can no longer look into each other's eyes or even look together in the same direction.

> While I was reproaching you your letter, my dear Muse, you were re-proaching yourself. You cannot believe how much that touched me, not because of the fact itself (I was sure that, after calm reflection, you would soon see things as I do), but because of the simultaneity of our conclusions. We are thinking in unison. Have you noticed it? If our bodies are far from each other, our souls touch. Mine is often with yours. It is a form of perception only achieved in lasting affections. *(July 15, 1853)*

The letters—written simply to reproach or complain—make them squint; luckily, between these letters, entrusted to the able hands of the postal service, their shared and unspoken thoughts realign their perspectives and are recorded only after the fact. What does Flaubert want? Thoughts and images that communicate themselves, a communion so intimate that writing is superfluous. His letters to Louise often express a nostalgia for this kind of relationship: "I had thought you kept me company in my own soul, and that there would be a great circle around the two of us, separating us from others" (December 14, 1853). Flaubert's fundamental epistolary objective is to communicate without letters: "I had thought it wasn't necessary to write to you." If he writes anyway, it is because he is in mourning for the magic circle inside which everything goes without saying. The initial visual moment of contact (in Pradier's studio) is over and has always been part of the past. Everything else, which should be equally easily and immediately understood, must now be explained.

Flaubert's letters to Louise attempt to rebuild their lost synchronicity of thought through dictation and indoctrination. His tone is often authoritative, sometimes even didactic (a tendency he notices himself, not without humor: "What a pity I am not a professor at the Collège de France" [August 26, 1853]). He describes himself at length—his ideas, tastes (especially distastes), moods, judgments—in order to win Louise over to his views, to make her think as he does and be as he is, in absolute complicity. There should be no difference between them, especially not the primordial difference between man and woman. The sentimental education he dictates is imperative on this point: "But what you dislike, perhaps, is precisely the fact that I treat you like a man and not like a woman. Try to put some of your intelligence into your relations with me" (September 28, 1846). Louise is wrong to think of herself as Flaubert's mistress and to emphasize the very differences between them that he tries to ignore and invalidate:

I should like to make of you something entirely apart—neither friend nor mistress. Each of those categories is too restricted, too exclusive—

one doesn't sufficiently love a friend, and one is too idiotic with a mistress. It is the intermediate term that I seek, the essence of those two sentiments combined. What I want, in short, is that, like a new kind of hermaphrodite, you give me with your body all the joys of the flesh and with your mind all those of the soul. *(September 28, 1846)*

To make of Louise something entirely apart, to separate her from the rest of the world, to remove her from her real identity so that she can keep him company inside the magic circle—this is, from the beginning, Flaubert's constant temptation. Six years later, nothing has changed. Louise continues to demand confessions of love, Flaubert is still less than obliging: "And I am going to say something that will seem strange to you. It does not seem to me that you are my mistress. Never does that banal term enter my mind when I think of you. In me you have a special place, which has never been occupied by anyone. If you were absent, it would remain empty" (December 11, 1852). Here he spells it out: Louise is not his mistress, she fills another, special place. She must project herself onto the same blank screen as Flaubert, superimposing his image on hers, making them one: "I would like us to keep our two bodies but have only one mind. All that I want of you, as a woman, is the flesh. Let the rest be mine, or better, be me, made on the same model, the same model" (March 27, 1853).

Flaubert blames the sexual difference for all other differences, for the misunderstandings, all the minor interferences that prevent them from seeing things in the same light. He tries constantly to invalidate the sexual difference—in the hope that without it, their lost complicity will be revived. Even his aesthetic debates circle around the basic denunciation of sexual difference. Fundamentally for Flaubert (and this is perhaps too schematic a statement), if Louise's thoughts are unclear, it is because she thinks as a woman. If she does not write well, it is because she writes with her sexuality. Flaubert is thus repeatedly obliged to correct her poems and to dole out lessons in poetics. Louise's failure is that she cannot separate art from her female passions.

She merges her self with her style. In everything she writes, she is undeniably a woman and thus will never be the perfect echo and accomplice Flaubert would like to make of her:

> Must I speak to you about art? Won't you accuse me of passing quickly over affairs of the heart? But in fact everything is bound up together, and what distorts your life is also distorting your style. For you continually alloy your concepts with your passions, and this weakens the first and prevents you from enjoying the second. Oh, if I could make you what I dream of! What a woman, what a human being, you would be! And first and foremost, how happy you would be! *(November 25, 1853)*

"If I could make you what I dream of": variations on a familiar theme. The incorruptible Flaubert indulges in a fit of blatant narcissism, Pygmalion emerging from beneath the churlish guise of the hermit of Croisset. Still, although he works desperately to make Louise over in his image, he makes little effort to render this image attractive and his self-portrait is, for the most part, relatively austere. The small part of his life that he spends with Louise reappears time and again in happy memories, but the rest is generally depicted as a withdrawal, an exile, immobile and impersonal, a succession of periods of mourning: the self-sacrifice he considers necessary for his rebirth as a writer (a new life in which Louise will no longer play much of a part). Making Louise over in his image means binding her to something that is hidden, to a personality destined to disappear. The self-portrait Flaubert paints in his letters is only slightly less repulsive than Kafka's. He foreshadows it in his second letter: "You would not believe me when I told you I was old." "The grandeur of your love fills me with humility; you deserved someone better than I." "I thought long and *very seriously* . . . of becoming a Mohammedan in Smyrna. The day will come when I will go and settle somewhere far from here, and nothing more will be heard of me" (August 6 or 7, 1846). This is only the beginning: Flaubert's battle for recognition in the nonlocation he chooses will be an extended one.

In order to conform to her lover's wishes, then, Louise must assimilate his desire for absence and withdrawal into her own character. She is also expected to acknowledge this desire in him, to give it substance, to accord it the strength of an act. Flaubert's epistolary program is not, ultimately, much more rewarding than Kafka's. In fact there is very little difference between the two. In both cases, the writers use letters to make the other acknowledge their disappearance or self-sacrifice, their absence. Ideally, they need a correspondent who will *support* this absence, be an accomplice to it and, in some way, identify with it. (Hence the incessant circulation of images, necessary for full identification to take place.) To lose your personality, you need someone for whom you are no longer a person. You need someone to whom you no longer talk, who can understand without words: someone who will join you in a telepathic dialogue of shadows and ghosts.

In countless cases, the letter writer becomes fundamentally a non-being, or a being nowhere, supported in his anonymity by his correspondent. Proust, Kafka, and Flaubert attach themselves to letters in order to lose themselves. Their faces and voices are lost in transit, without return addresses. They become invisible in the images they circulate. Proust hides in the nocturnal fog of his fumigations; Kafka sends greetings from his cellar; Flaubert plays the renegade in Smyrna-on-Seine. Letters have been, for all three, an exercise in disappearance as well as an apprenticeship in displacement and representation. Letters have also been, perhaps, a necessary rung on the ladder to fiction, to the required strength of imagination and projection. You must begin as no one, as a pure force of movement (best exemplified by Baudelaire's poet-wanderer in *Les foules*), if you are to project yourself into the other characters, times, and places that are the stuff of novels. It is doubtless no coincidence that, of all the writers discussed here, it is the novelists who remain most absent from their images or who are the most obsessed by the idea of understanding without words. After all, the work of the novelist is an act of understanding, generalized and extended to all others, to an entire humanity that must be reimagined or reinvented, made up of characters also understood without verbal communication. At least if we believe Flaubert, who sees in the novelist's projection his own form of charity: "No, we are not good; but this faculty of assimilating all miseries and of imagining oneself suffering through them is perhaps the true human charity. Tke oneself the center of humanity, to work to be its genet, where all its scattered veins meet" (June 6, 1853). "e other hand, no one has breathed others in as deepave. I have inhaled the smells of unknown manure. Ielt compassion for many things that do not touch th sensitive people" (May 8, 1852). From the corresponde with Louise—an act of aspiration rather than in-spirationnd in return for all of its demands on the imagination, have ome Emma, Rodolphe, and Léon.

Caroline Chérie

The epistolary genre, with its reliance on images, is an experiment in distortion and loss, a commerce of absence. Letters are often an initia-tion into a state of mourning (for oneself as much as for the other). At the same time, they place the letter writer in a position beyond all possibility of "real" grief. The epistolary imagination feeds on fune-real imagery, a dependence that is most obvious in Flaubert's case. One must see that the letters to Louise Colet are written as a substi-tute for Flaubert's real mourning for Caroline Flaubert-Hamard, his sister, who died on March 20, 1846 (two months after his father and two months after giving birth to her daughter, Caroline Hamard).

On March 25, after his sister's burial, Flaubert confides in Maxime du Camp:

> In the morning, when everything was done, I gave her a long last fare-well kiss in her coffin. I bent over her, and as I lowered my head into the coffin I felt the lead buckle under my hands. It was I who attended to the casts. I saw the great paws of those louts touching her and cov-ering her with plaster. I shall have her hands and her face. I shall ask

Pradier to make me her bust and will put it in my room. I have her big colored shawl, a lock of her hair, her table and writing-desk. That is all—all that remains of those we love!

Three months later he meets Louise Colet, in Pradier's studio, but his mind remains elsewhere—in Caroline's coffin, no doubt. He comes to commission the bust of his sister, to create a final image of her, and he leaves with Louise, who will become the essential element in the remembrance to which he consecrates himself.

A letter from 1852, written after Pradier's death, confirms the sculptor's position as a link in the chain between Caroline and Louise. His death reminds Flaubert simultaneously of Caroline's death and of the first meeting with Louise:

It is six years ago this month that we met at his house. Poor man! I have been dumbfounded all day by the news. I could fill a whole volume with obituaries for the people I've known who have died. When you're young, you associate the future realization of your dreams with the people who surround you. Then as they disappear one by one, the dreams disappear with them. I felt this already with my sister, the charming woman I never speak of because a certain modesty of emotion seals my lips. I buried many ambitions with her, almost all of my worldly desire for glory. I had raised her—she had a solid and astute mind that charmed me. *(to Louise Colet, June 9, 1852)*

Death, like eating, occurs frequently in Flaubert's writing. Death begets death, and every new grief serves as a reminder of the previous ones. Flaubert's book of obituaries is full of associations. Death has countless roots and offshoots. Pradier's death recalls Caroline's six years earlier,[4] and Flaubert does not hesitate to remind Louise of this fact: the love story that began in 1846 in Pradier's studio also marked the end of a much older story. Or perhaps beginning the new story was simply a way to avoid ending the old one, a means of prolonging the mourning. Louise filled Caroline's empty seat—not replacing her (Flaubert is inconsolable), but giving substance to her absence. So long as Louise maintains her distance and restricts herself to epistolary communication, she embodies and keeps alive a disappearance that would otherwise be gradually forgotten.

While Flaubert's relationship with Louise is ruled by absence and distance, his relationship with Caroline was extremely rich. Caroline seems to be the only being who could inspire in Flaubert a desire for presence. After her death in 1846, Flaubert goes into permanent mourning for this presence. He mourns completeness (narcissistically, perhaps) and the image or alter ego in which he could recognize and love himself. Without Caroline, he has no ambition, no "wordly desire for glory." All that he has left of Caroline is a shawl, a lock of hair, a table, a desk: a poor exchange if we see that, dying, she took with her his personality and any desire he might have had to be someone. When he buries Caroline, he buries the successful image of himself that he had created for her. It is this buried image that he presents to Louise for countersignature and endorsement. He appoints Louise the guardian of the grave he has dug for himself—and from which he will later be resurrected as the impersonalized Flaubert.

The letter written after Pradier's death stresses the educational role that Flaubert played in Caroline's life. He writes of how he raised, educated, and formed her into the possessor of, as he puts it, "a solid and astute mind that charmed me." If there is some Pygmalion in Flaubert's nature, it manifests itself the most clearly in his relationship with Caroline. And the authoritative character of his letters to Louise—the aesthetic and ethical guidelines he tries to impose on her—is perhaps only the disproportionate shadow of his lost pedagogical happiness with Caroline. Deprived of the only audience that meant something to him, all he has left to offer Louise is a paradoxical lesson on solitude, exile, and impersonality, forever haunted by the complicity and unity he has lost.

From the beginning of his correspondence with Louise, Flaubert insists not only on his attraction to exile, but also on his desire for withdrawal from his audience. What he writes is not intended to be read, perhaps not even by Louise, and it is only out of weakness that he, once, gives in to the impulse to read something to her:

> When I was a child I dreamed of fame like everyone else, no more nor less; in me good sense sprouted late, but it is firmly planted. So it is very doubtful that the public will ever have occasion to read a single line written by me; if this happens, it will not be before ten years, at least. I don't know what led me to read you something; forgive that weakness. I could not resist the temptation to make you think highly of me. But I was sure of success, wasn't I? What puerility on my part! *(August 8–9, 1846)*[5]

Glory, readers, admiration: such are the dreams of a child, buried with Caroline, his only real reader for years. "Thus in eight days or so I will be back with you, ready for my old antics, pranks, and jokes" (to Caroline, April 16, 1842). "In three weeks, you will see me return, more eager than ever to continue my performances, because I have missed my audience" (to Caroline, November 16, 1842). Flaubert was Caroline's happy fool, her personal clown. When he warns Louise (in his second letter) not to delude herself about their relationship, he explains immediately: "My basic character, whatever anyone may say, is that of the clown" (August 6 or 7, 1846). Unfortunately, he is now nobody's clown. His audience has widowed and orphaned him, and he has no one left to watch him, to love him, or to make him love the many images of himself he used to project for Caroline.

The complicity between Flaubert and his sister was so complete that it even survived her marriage with Hamard:

> How nice your letter was, dear sister, nice and simple as you are, my little pet. I could almost see you in it, with your messy, curly hair and the little dimple in your chin; speaking of which, I hope I will see you again in haircurlers. I have no one left to throttle with my two hands while yelling, "good old rat, good old rat" . . . When you are here, if you like, we can begin a play. You will roll on my bed again like the dog, and I will play the Negro, "yes, I like my mistress, like mistress." *(July 10, 1845)*

Both are over twenty years old, one of them married, but he is still her clown, dreaming of games of make-believe; she is still his rat, his

128

good old Carolo who writes him the same nice letters as before. When Flaubert arrives at Pradier's studio, he is reeling from the loss of this relationship, and he replays it by binding himself to Louise. Louise confirms the loss and, in some way, hides behind the absent Caroline, supporting the image Flaubert wants so desperately to recapture. But the figure between them condemns all new attempts at complicity to failure. Flaubert sometimes tells Louise this, probably without really realizing what he is saying or that he is, to use his own expression, carrying with him the corpse of his Siamese twin: "Our wishes and desires always coincide. In love, we are attached to each other like Siamese twins, two bodies with one soul. But if one dies before the other, the survivor must drag a corpse along behind him" (September 4–5, 1846).

Is Flaubert thinking of Louise when he writes this or of his sister, whose absence he carries with him everywhere? Is there a difference between the two? It is difficult, especially in his first letters, to separate his grief from his passion. He makes some delicate attempts to avoid the confusion, but they are always somewhat ambiguous: "I am not writing to you on my ordinary writing-paper—that is edged with black and I want nothing sad to pass from me to you" (August 4–5, 1846). He reminds her that his paper is bordered in black, in case she has forgotten his loss, but he adds that he won't use it for letters to her, as if he were keeping it for impossible letters to Caroline. Or as if it is really someone else who is writing to Louise. Who exactly is Flaubert anyway? Didn't he disappear with Caroline? Aren't his letters to Louise simply an announcement of his mourning for himself? Aren't they the necessary stage of self-sacrifice on his way to becoming an impersonal subject, the creator of great works of art? His first love letter is, granted, not bordered in black, but its sentiments are. It is, like the letters that follow, preoccupied with mourning. His "I want nothing sad to pass from me to you" is ironic when we consider that there is rarely anything even remotely light-hearted in Flaubert's letters. Mourning is the most consistent motif in Flaubert's intimacies:

"In my soul I have already attended a thousand funerals," he writes a few days later, with his legendary cheer (August 9, 1846). Flaubert's soul, as Abraham and Torok would say, has become a crypt. Built on loss, it has taken out a lifetime's subscription to absence. Louise's letters must replace Caroline's presence. He says it himself so directly that there is little need to discuss it further: "I won't put your letters in a little pouch as you do, but in my sister's writing desk which I will keep on the table where I gave her lessons" (September 17, 1846).

A postscript's worth of discussion anyway. In Flaubert's last letter to Louise (before the final breaking-up note in 1855): "Where do you find that I have lost 'the meaning of certain emotions that I no longer feel'? First of all, I do feel them. I have a *human* heart, and if I don't want a child, it's because I am already too *paternal*. I love my little niece as if she were my daughter, and I look after her enough *(actively)* to prove that these are not just words" (April 22, 1854). Flaubert will never be a father to anyone, especially not to the children Louise is regularly afraid of bearing him (or does she actually hope for them?). His name will die with him, if it cannot die before then. His only children are the ones he does not have, those created in thought, recreated later in novels: "I often think tenderly of unknown beings, the unborn, strangers, etc., who are moved or will be moved by the same things as me. Books turn all of humanity into an eternal family. All the people who live in your thought become children seated at your table" (to Louise, March 25, 1854; this letter is written shortly before the last to her). Caroline, Flaubert's cherished sister, was his first true child of the mind. And eight years later it is Caroline, his niece, who revives his desire to teach. Is it purely a coincidence that his last letter to Louise refers to this rebirth? Flaubert travels full circle from Caroline Flaubert-Hamard to Caroline Hamard. Flaubert's paternity is assured without much effort on his part (the child does not even bear his name), and his Colet parenthesis can be closed. Caroline Hamard's attention allows him finally to accept the loss of his first audience, Caroline Flaubert. And Louise's absence—which served as a constant reminder of the loss of Caroline—no longer serves any real purpose.

Condolences

In *La carte postale,* Jacques Derrida notes that the idea of destination contains within it the idea of death: "If I say that I am writing to a person who is dead, not to someone who will be dead, but who is dead already by the time I finish my sentence, I am not playing. Genet said that his plays were addressed to the dead, and I mean it the way he did as I continue writing at this rate, endlessly, to you."[6] Perhaps more than any other form of writing, the epistolary genre (one that Derrida uses—or imitates—in the first part of the book) is an experiment that relies on the lethal charge carried by all attempts at destination. It is our favorite way of speaking to the dead, of passing from Kafka's "human intercourse" to an exchange of shadows, reflections, and ghosts.

Flaubert's letters to Caroline via Louise are a perfect example of this attempted epistolary relationship with the dead. On another level, in echo to Jean Genet's declaration, there is the dedication of Baudelaire's *Paradis artificiels,* addressed to a mysterious J.G.F. (whose identity no one has ever managed to establish definitively):

> Whether or not the reason for this dedication is understood makes very little difference to me. Is it really necessary for the happiness of the author that his book be understood by anyone other than the man or woman for whom it was composed? Is it, in truth, indispensable that it be written for *someone?* As for me, I have now so little taste for the living world that, like those sensitive and idle women who make their confidences to imaginary friends, I would be happy to write only for the dead.

Baudelaire would be happy to write only for the dead and makes little effort to be understood by his living audience. The dead are the ideal, imagined readers of his poetry. His letters, on the other hand, seem

131

to testify more to the irritating impossibility of avoiding the living, especially his tenacious mother. In Baudelaire's correspondence (with his mother and the other creditors who follow in her footsteps), there is a strange shortage of death—and consequently a shortage of imagination and identification, of images, of "I think of you." Baudelaire's letters are implacably prosaic because death, between his mother and himself, must be avoided at all costs. Neither of the two, as we have seen, has the right to die first. Neither of them can imagine or foresee the absence of the other.

Baudelaire would be happy to write only for the dead, but his living mother constantly demands explanations. Yet his mother is the one person to whom his texts are *not* addressed. Everything poetic that Baudelaire writes is intended for the dead, never to be read by his mother—intended, in effect, to counteract her living presence. On the other hand, every letter he writes is addressed to his mother, in one way or another. She becomes a symbol of all the living who refuse to die. Baudelaire's correspondence once again serves exactly the opposite purpose of his poetic work. It is the price exacted for his refusal to address the living elsewhere.

But it is undeniably Proust who makes the most systematic use of the epistolary genre as an entry into active mourning. While he implicitly mourns *all* the correspondents he never sees and can only imagine, he never writes as regularly and as conscientiously as to those who are actually suffering some bereavement.

Proust specializes in condolence letters. They are his compromise on the impossible route to a real dialogue with the dead. It is as if expressing condolences is the deepest form of truth. In all of his letters, someone is (either implicitly or explicitly) lost or feared lost; there is always a corpse of some form or other. Some people he corresponds with *only* when he can associate himself with their mourning. All you have to do to get a letter from Marcel Proust is lose a loved one (if a threat to your own life is impossible to arrange), and it will arrive in the next mail—even if Proust has never even heard of the dearly departed: "But isn't whatever is yours to some extent mine? I weep with infinite bitterness for him though I did not know him; I rebel against his death, I hope for a miracle which will be revealed in the letter that arrives, and then I realize the impossibility of it, and I think of you again, and weep again" (to Marie Nordlinger, October 18, 1908).

Proust feels closest to his friends—or closer than he had previously suspected—when they have just lost or are threatened with the loss of a friend or loved one: "Because I love you very much, little Robert, and I love your wife even more than I knew, more than I knew her, so to speak, since I have greatly sympathised with her suffering from afar" (to Robert de Billy, October 1908). Nothing draws people closer than definitive separations, whether imagined or real.

On the other hand, the dead make the loved ones who survive them even more lovable (which is lucky, considering that it is easier to sympathize, in the original sense of the word, with those who are left than with those who have disappeared). Unable to write to the dead, Proust writes to those who mourn them, transferring his affection for the dead to their survivors. At times he even confuses his bereaved friends with the friends they have lost, and his condolence letters often address the dead by proxy. The living and the dead exist, for Proust, in close proximity, almost overlapping. (He is, once again, obsessed with metonymy.) Who does Proust love more, Eugène Fould or Madame Fould, his recently deceased mother? On March 24, 1911, the mother seems to come out on top: "Above all, I don't want you to think that I, who loved your mother so and who will mourn her all my life, have not felt any pain." The night before, however, his affection was directed more toward Eugène (perhaps it was exhausted then, since he does not address another letter to Fould for six years): "I couldn't talk to you just now in that crowd of people. And at the moment, dear friend, I feel that there are forms of pain which break the pen as they break the voice. I feel much pain. I have never loved you as much as now when I see you so unhappy. My poor fellow, I loved her too and this was a bolt from the blue" (March 23, 1911). A bolt from the blue: there is no better way to describe the sudden onset of Proust's double affection.

The "I couldn't talk to you" is also worth noting. True condolences are silent, like the grief they try to echo and ally themselves with. Telepathy is an integral part of sympathy. Condolence letters are intended to transmit a permanent and silent compassion for their recipient, a tacit and eternal involvement in the loss. They fall, perhaps more than any other kind of letter, within the realm of representation and imagination. The omnipresent "I'm thinking of you" in Proust's letters is always a form of condolence, an acknowledgment of a disappearance or absence. Nothing excites his imagination quite so much as the sufferings of others.[7] Somebody else's loss is a source of imaginative possibility because sharing in it always begins with some kind of identification. And perhaps this is the most interesting part of the process for Proust: filling the empty spaces left behind by the disappearances of others.

Still, the problem with identifying with another's grief is that the compassion is never quite complete. Some things are imaginable, others remain hidden:

> I don't know anything about you—and yet I know too much, because when I think of you, which is all the time, I have the same feeling as in jealousy, though there's no connection. I mean that, without knowing anything precisely, I keep imagining everything best calculated to torture me, at every moment I see you either so shaken by sobs that it drives me to despair or so terrifyingly calm that it depresses me not to see you weeping, for that might comfort you a little. *(to Antoine Bibesco, who has just lost his mother, November 10, 1902)*

One can never completely identify with the bereaved, never suffer *for* them quite enough, and this in itself becomes another source of suffering: "I suffer a lot at not being able to be with you" (to Gaston de Caillavet, who has also just lost his mother, January 13, 1910). The other's pain that Proust tries to adopt is succeeded by the pain of not being able to adopt it. The fluctuations between contemplating what he knows already and the desire to know more are endless. Proust will never satisfy his curiosity, for example, about the death of Georges de Lauris' mother. Even knowing all there is to know, he is avid for more: "I know your mother so well that you cannot tell me anything about her which I do not know already, nor tell me anything that I do not listen to not merely with interest and sympathy, but with a truly painful avidity. You know Georges that I don't think of anything else anymore and that my need to see you is just now above all a need to hear you talk of her" (shortly after February 18, 1907).

The adoption of another's mourning also causes personal suffering—a feeling of powerlessness and an inability to comprehend the loss. And this failure provides Proust with another entry into mourning, no doubt one of the reasons he takes such painstaking care with his condolence letters. First he expresses all the sympathy he can muster, then he is pained (or pleasured) by its limits and inadequacy: I want to reach the source of pain, and I succeed precisely *because* I can never quite reach it. Another's imagined mourning is always hypothetical. The reality of it matters little, so long as the attempt to identify with it fails.[8] It can be replaced by any equivalent pain Proust chooses, provided that it is *unimaginably* painful and that its full extent escapes him. The actual mourning can be replaced, for example, with the thoughts of Albertine's perverse and unknown pleasures that torment Marcel—pleasures so close to pain that the two blend together. It is only a short step from sympathy to jealousy, a step Proust takes quite easily in the letter to Bibesco (1902) quoted above. (Granted, he qualifies it with a "though there's no connection"—but then who else would have made one?) And what if the pain one feels for a friend who has lost his mother creates the same sensation as the jealous fantasies about a mistress' private pleasures?

Suffering is, in his countless condolence letters, Proust's fundamental mode of existence.[9] It is as if he lives only through his painfully incomplete and impossible identification with others' grief, as if his entire existence were a kind of inadequate projection. A specialist of suffering is also a man who suffers, doomed to botch the suffering he is destined for, or to attain it through this failure. The fugitive is the shadow cast by the suffering being; Proust grasps at others' pain, the reflection of his own pain and his most intimate double, without ever being able to unite with it.

A specialist of suffering who suffers himself, Proust travels untiringly from one sorrow to the next down a long trail of condolence letters. Periods of mourning punctuate his existence. The dead are what make him live. His knowledge of pain—or perhaps just his desire to know it—is what makes him a writer, and it is doubtless in quest of this knowledge that he attaches himself to the recently bereaved: "How I would like to see you, I am so saddened by your sorrow that my company would cause neither of us any discomfort" (to Madame Scheikevitch, January 9, 1915). He invites himself wherever there has been a death (symbolically, of course, since he keeps his physical distance). He makes it clear that his presence would be no trouble at all—he is familiar with death; he knows how to experience pain quietly and appropriately and to join the deceased in thought, since they are the only people who really live for him. "The dead are alive for me," he writes a little later to the recently widowed Madame de Caillavet (April 23, 1915).

Proust passes from one death to another through letters. Time after time he proves his knowledge of grief. His own experience draws him closer to those in mourning and enables him to learn more about the suffering that makes them so interesting to him: "Everybody is shattered, but no one can feel the same sorrow as I feel, because no one has hoped and felt with you so much" (to Georges de Lauris, February 18, 1907). No one can sympathize better than the ever-suffering Proust, who is so close to the dead. He knows what it's all about; he is an expert on funeral services. If you have lost a friend or relative, Proust, who speaks *for* the dead, will not only console you but will also help you to find them. He will initiate you into a form of dialogue with the dearly departed, as he suggests in this letter to Robert Dreyfus (who has just lost a brother and whom Proust encourages knowingly to continue his writing): "Anyway, by continuing to live in this way, you will live in your own world where the barriers of flesh and time do not exist, where death does not exist because neither time nor flesh exist, where you can live sweetly in the immortal company of those you love" (November 10, 1910). A few years earlier, Proust consoled Georges de Lauris in the same way, by pointing out the paradoxical benefits of his mother's death: "There is one thing I can tell you now: you will know a sweetness that you cannot yet conceive. When you had your mother you thought a great deal about the days when you would no longer have her. When you have become accustomed to the terrible experience of being forever thrown back on the past, then you will feel her gently returning to life, coming back to take her place again, her whole place, beside you" (February 18, 1907).

These two letters owe much to the death of Proust's own mother in 1905. He continues his relentless mourning for her through his friends' losses and never finds them so worthy of his affection as when recently orphaned. Proust himself draws the analogy in de Lauris' case: "I feel as if I were losing Mama for a second time" (February 16, 1907). The reassuring idea of communication with the dead appears, for the first time, in reference to his own mother: "the perfect communion I lived in with Mamma was not broken by her death, as I have never let a minute go by without thinking of her, even when asleep, or without seeing her always beside me, or asking her opinion of all that I do and believing I hear her answers" (to L. Landowski, June 8, 1906). While mourning (or perhaps not mourning) his mother, Proust becomes an expert on relations with the dead. It must be noted, however, that he has always been one. If the "perfect communion" between Proust and his mother continues after 1905, it is because their communication always occured within the realm of death. Madame Proust's actual disappearance has no real effect on her relationship with her son.

Independent of body, voice, or presence, the "voice of the heart," which Proust tries to echo in all of his letters, can be seen as a repeated address to the dead, an address to Madame Proust (who plays the opposite role for Proust as Madame Aupick did for Baudelaire). Merely receiving a letter from Proust places you somewhere outside the world of the living. And this is what makes his condolence letters seem symptomatic of something far more important.

Proust's mourning for his mother begins long before her death. She is always the symbolic presence against which he fights for absence, as an army fights for ground. As such, she is the source of his epistolary urges for distance. Her actual death has sometimes been considered an "epistemological" cut-off point. It has been seen as the event that allowed Proust to write—as if her disappearance finally gave his writing some destination, an addressee—if only in a profanatory mode, as Jean-Louis Baudry has suggested.[10] After a close reading of the correspondence, however, this conclusion seems a little too deterministic, if only because of the profound unity of tone in the letters. There is no difference between the letters dated before 1905 and those written later. All are marked by the same mourning of the other, by the same "I think of you." The important letter written in 1902 on the death of Antoine Bibesco's mother more than proves the early development of his talent. So does a letter to Armand de Guiche, dated a few weeks before the fatal September 26, 1905, the first in a long repetitive series:

> Later you will perhaps want to see me. To think that your Mother realized, perhaps, that she was leaving you, believed perhaps that never, *never,* in all of *eternity* would she see *you* again, you who were all her happiness in life, it is that thought that kills me. I know through Mathieu that your brother is ill with grief. I cannot tell you how much sympathy that makes me feel for him. As for you, dear friend, I love you

a thousand times more than ever, if that's possible, since I have become so intimately absorbed by your immense pain. *(July 18, 1905)*

Proust clearly never misses an opportunity to imagine his forthcoming sorrow, to anticipate his own mourning through the excruciating suffering of others. His correspondence is not suddenly marked by mourning in 1905. It always has been and always will be, as if death (his mother's or anyone else's) never happens often enough. It is hard to see Madame Proust's death as a determining factor in his writing simply because her death does not occur, for Proust, on one exact date. It is diffuse, disseminated, without beginning or end. It accompanies Marcel to his own deathbed. For a long time Proust has practiced his mother's death, the most surprising thing, perhaps, being his willingness to admit this fact in a letter to Barrès:

> All our lives we had been practising—she had been teaching me to do without her in preparation for the day when she would leave me, ever since my childhood when she used to refuse ten times in a row to come and say goodnight before going out . . . All those anxieties cured by a few words on the telephone, or her visit to Paris, or one kiss from her, with what strength I feel them now when I know that nothing will calm them. And, for my part, I had been trying to persuade her that I could live very well without her. *(January 19, 1906)*

Madame Proust and her son practice daily for each other's deaths in an attempt to understand the suffering they will cause (and how to cause that suffering). Letters are unquestionably the textbooks for their training. But, by practicing pain—in the paradoxical hope that this will make it more bearable when it actually comes—they become more and more bound to it. They become its subjects. Their apprenticeship will never end, and they probably understand this from the beginning. Madame Proust's death, when it does arrive, leaves Proust in the grip of an immeasurable sorrow. In addition to his own loss, he suffers great remorse at having made his mother foresee his own suffering so clearly:

I have now the double torture of thinking that she must have known, with such anxiety, that she was leaving me, and thinking that the last days of her life were so afflicted, so constantly preoccupied by worries about my health. I will feel this remorse forever and it will spoil not only all joy in my life—if I can ever find any again—but also the sweetness of her memory and of the delicious life we led together, when, of the two, it was me who was pitied when I was so happy, so egotistically happy, rejoicing at her gentleness which hid so much sadness. *(to Maurice Barrès, January 19, 1906)*

His preparations for mourning have thus doubly failed: first because Madame Proust, in spite of everything, keeps her final pain to herself, without her son ever really knowing whether she has experienced it. ("She must have known that she was leaving me": Proust experiences exactly the same torture he felt at the death of Madame de Guiche, several weeks earlier.) And second because she takes his pain with her, the pain that was so delicious for him as long as it was *shared* with her.

The fundamental result of Madame Proust's death (if there is one) is that Proust loses his main image of suffering. He can no longer imagine or appropriate it. And in this loss, he discovers pain's most profound characteristic—that it escapes, that it cannot be lived in the present. Where pain truly begins, life ends. "I cause suffering, therefore I am," we read in his letter to Gide. The more complete statement would be, "I cause my mother to suffer, therefore I am." Proust loses, with his mother, the depository of his own pain, the possibility of finding and knowing himself through the pain he causes her. Pain becomes less familiar to him because it is more distant. Who will read his health bulletins now? There will never be another person who knows so well how to suffer for him and because of him.

Thus, long before Albertine, suffering is the fugitive in Proust's life. He is constantly *à la recherche de la douleur perdue*, stolen away by his mother. He follows it from loss to loss, from mourning to mourning; and, always a disciple of metonymy, he looks for it in those who were closest to his late mother's pain, just as Marcel turns to Albertine's friends and accomplices for the truth about her pleasures. During his search Proust uncovers one of his mother's notebooks describing her own bereavements. We can only imagine what this discovery must have meant to Proust. (For us, it sheds light on Proust's fascination with suffering—it was apparently a family trait.) After finding the notebook—in which her name is mentioned—Proust begins writing to Madame de Noailles again, a correspondent he has neglected for years:

> Have I told you that I recently found a notebook in which Mamma had told the stories of her father's, her mother's and Papa's last illnesses, hour by hour, stories which, without having the least intention of implying anything, are marked by such distress that one finds it difficult to go on living after having read them. One name is mentioned, one thought transcribed: yours; one thought of you, of your wondering face. It is an obscure but heartrending, and for me, great, form of glory. *(June 3, 1912)*

He feels suddenly close to Madame de Noailles because his mother was close to her when facing the loss of her loved ones. He writes also to Ladislas Landowski, his mother's doctor (the specialist of her suffering). Madame Proust and Landowski become one and the same person for Proust, through their familiarity with her pain. Writing to Landowski brings her briefly back to life, as if her existence depended only on the physical pain she suffered:

> I didn't want to send you my book earlier because it would have meant speaking to you, in my letter and especially in my book, of other things, before having had the chance to speak to you of Mamma, or to tell you that not one day, not one hour, since she left me, ruining my life forever, *have I ceased thinking of you and at the same time of her, confusing my gratitude to you with my tenderness for her.* But precisely because of that, because of the terrible place you have occupied in my heart since that time, it seemed very painful to think that even just a few pages of mine could appear without the person who occupies my best and deepest thoughts having received them. *(June 8, 1906; my italics)*

Proust's remembrance of pain past is unquestionably the source of his epistolary urges, and probably of his other writings as well. Could we not read all of *La recherche* as an attempt to capture what letters cannot, to depict pain in all its fleeting beauty? When you have dedicated your life to suffering, what can you do but write? What can you do but remember and recreate the pain and sorrow that you never experienced quite satisfactorily in life? Writing unites Proust's penchants for mourning and for passion. Read in this light, it is no longer necessary to choose between the deaths of Madame Proust and Agostinelli as the source of *La recherche*. Albertine symbolizes *all* lost suffering, and Agostinelli and Madame Proust meet in her character—or, more precisely, do not manage to meet. Marcel's pain is inspired by the pleasure he will never understand because the only person capable of explaining it to him has disappeared.

The true union of pleasure and pain in Proust's work comes only in *Le temps retrouvé:* Jupien's brothel and Charlus in chains, whom Marcel studies so intently through his oeil-de-boeuf that one thinks he might have taken Charlus' place (the identification becomes part of the syntax of the passage).[11] This union marks the beginning of the end. A few pages later, in the unevenly paved courtyard of the hotel des Guermantes, Marcel becomes a writer. The book to come is the suffering to come.

Beyond the Living and the Dead

All these attempts at epistolary communication ultimately pose one and the same problem: correspondents are always too alive, too present. Kafka, Proust, and Flaubert would much prefer to write to the dead, and they try repeatedly to turn their correspondents into silent, absent images. Letters walk the fine line between the living and the dead that writer after writer works to twist and obscure.

Hence the profound affinity between letters and literature, which is rarely addressed to one particular other and is always based on the disappearance or destruction of the other as individual. (Without this foundation, literature would lose its universal quality. As it is, almost anyone can find personal relevance in the literary text.) Literary discourse relies on the ability to speak to the dead (and also, to some extent, on the sentiment Pascal Quignard expressed a few years ago, "I hope to be read in 1640"). Literature emerges from the loss of the other. The epistolary genre, in turn, never stops inspiring, exploring, and testing this loss. Letters are necessarily a preparation for mourning, and thus they are often an initiation into writing.

Artaud's letters from Rodez cannot be strictly defined as either literature or letters because they radically alter the border between the two. If, when they were written, it was impossible not to see them as a literary act, sometimes even as the essence of literature itself, it was precisely because the line between the living and the dead was as fuzzy as that between the literary and nonliterary. The two distinctions are equally vague, and perhaps they are equivalent.

Artaud writes countless letters from Rodez to protest the evil spell that has been placed on him. As discussed above, however, he expects his correspondents to understand his complaints without having to read the letters. When it does become necessary to address them, they fall on the side of language, and of the Other, in an alien and hostile world. If Artaud has to write to them, they are no longer the perfect partners he dreams of, the friends who defend him without prompting. In a letter accusing his editor Henri Parisot of having fallen under the spell and not taking him seriously, Artaud specifies: "And anyway, I am not alone, but have always had around me a limited but faithful group of girls, of souls determined to love me and who are my partisans. They are in France, in Ireland, in Germany, in Mexico, in Afghanistan and in Cambodia, they are in Bali and perhaps also in Japan" (October 5, 1945). On one side, he has his "interlocutors" who need constant goading, on the other his "partisans," kindred souls who love him stubbornly, without questions or words, to whom any letter seems superfluous. With them, letters give way to telepathic communication. Artaud's correspondents are forced to choose between taking their place in language, among his enemies, or becoming "souls" on the planetary, telepathic network devoted to his defense and to his protest against the Other.

Whether the recipients of his letters write back is of little importance; whether they are alive or dead also matters little. The distinction is pointless and the eventual death of his correspondents holds no interest for Artaud. His letters are primarily addressed to the dead, whose immortal, speechless, partisan souls have survived them. Anie Besnard, for example: "Is it true that you are married. Some have even told me you were no longer of this world, but dead, no, because the soul of little Anie as I knew her and as I see her still will always survive in my heart" (February 27, 1946). Artaud will not give you up just because you happen to be dead. His epistolary noise is intended to wake the dead, and being "no longer of this world" does not release you from your duties as his correspondent. It would be far too easy to take advantage of your death to wash your hands of his fate, and if you are dead, it is because you are *playing* dead. You are trying, in bad faith or under the force of some evil spell, to forget him. A little good will and you can connect directly with his soul, as he does with yours—beyond the reach of the diabolical double who has claimed your body. To Anie Besnard he writes: "I know that you are no longer yourself because you left to meet me last October 14 and, having left the Gare d'Orléans, you never came back and the woman I am writing to and who is called Anie Besnard is only a double produced by the demons and responsible for preventing me from finding little Anie's soul that I hear whistling and lisping everywhere" (October 6, 1945).

"I know that you are no longer yourself": I am not writing to you, as you are now, but to the person you used to be. I will find you again where you disappeared, where you were lost trying to find me. In the meantime I will write to your evil double, a zombie or impostor, to expose its deception:

I who loved you and still love your soul as if it were my little sister I have never stopped thinking of you for a single day during the three years since I last saw you or had news from you, but the marvellous soul I saw in you and that still exists, I wonder if you, Anie Besnard, still have it.— When you give in to Evil you believe yourself unchanged but you change, you become little by little another person, all that made up your soul disappears, and one day you realize this but you are then only a double of your former self, a Double, and that is how demons are formed. *(February 10, 1944)*

Behind the impostor—and even as the latter is being denounced— there still exists the ideal, subtracted addressee. The ideal addressee is what remains of the "official addressee" after the language and life necessary for communication have been removed. Real life begins with the death of language and its subjects (who are all mere doubles). It begins where the speaking double retreats, yielding its place to the authentic soul that Artaud alone can fully make over, in the image of his brothers in paranoia. (From the Misanthrope through Rousseau to President Schreber: there are many, each one unique and, of course, solitary.) Like them, Artaud is the last man alive in a world that has been destroyed, corrupted, peopled with botched, carelessly made beings, demonic shadows fighting to silence him. Artaud's prophetic gesticulations, his fury and rages, are all part of his battle for the fate of humanity (no more, no less) and of the human soul—the seeds of life that must be saved from the demons of language.

So in Artaud's letters we pass far beyond the question of his relationship with others; beyond the distinction between the living and the dead. Granted, he writes to the living, but only to tell them that they have been possessed, that their real selves have died. They are puppets animated in a theater that has taken the real world's place. And when he contemplates his correspondents' deaths, he lets them know that they will always be alive for him. "The dead are alive for me," writes Proust, meaning that his life continues *as if* the dead were still alive (he knows full well that they have escaped him—this is the tragedy and the saving grace of his life). For Artaud, the *as if* is lost, and he takes each figurative statement literally. The dead have not escaped him. They are even the only ones who truly live for him. The living are dead to his efforts. His fascination with language is thus linked to his desire to realize the old dream of communion with the dead—an inspiration, perhaps, behind every poetic work since Orpheus—or, more generally, his desire for a communion between souls that transcends language.

For Artaud to create literature, he has to write to someone or, more exactly, to a soul he will never forget. So, while the Rodez letters are far more radical than the letters to Rivière, the stakes are the same: literature born, in spite of itself, of letters. And if Rivière is no longer a stimulus or inspiration, his successor at the *NRF,* Jean Paulhan, is also in need of a recall to his own soul:

> We have had many thoughts together over the eight years since I last saw you, and we have spoken together many times across the distance and the space, and your soul and Jeanne Paulhan's soul have answered me fluidly in the atmosphere as if they were just a few meters from me in the waves emananting from my chest . . . and I have received from you and from Jeanne Paulhan a certain number of words from the heart which you haven't repeated in your letter, not because your letters have no heart, they are overflowing with it, but not the same kind of heart that has appeared each day and each time we have spoken one to one across space and *time*—but because you have been made spitefully to forget these words of the heart, in order to make you spitefully forget that the soul speaks in space, and that the souls of those who love each other answer each other across space as your soul answered mine that Sunday morning, September 10, at ten o'clock, with the soul of Jeanne Paulhan.

From June 5, 1923, to September 10, 1945, and later, Artaud makes no more distinction between the living and the dead than he does between literature and letters. Everything he writes is written exclusively for the immortal soul.

chapter four

The Letter, the Book

The Private Exchange

On September 9, 1898, Mallarmé died in Valvins, suffocated by a glottal spasm. Valéry was desolate. He wrote to tell Gide, "My dear fellow, I am prostrate. Mallarmé died yesterday morning." Gide did not get all the details until the day after the burial: "My dear André, here are the details. Writing them down will relieve me a bit, since for the last three nights I haven't slept, I've been crying like a child and suffocating" (September 12, 1898). In order not to choke like Mallarmé, Valéry entrusts his grief to Gide, beginning with the memory of their last meeting:

> All that is irreplaceable. Six or seven weeks ago, I spent the day there. He seemed to me weary—he was all white—and his little boat, still roped up and floating, was, he told me, forsaken. We went to his room to talk. He showed me some drafts of his *Hérodiade* in progress, etc., changed his undershirt in front of me, gave me water for my hands and then perfumed me with his perfume. In the evening he and his daughter accompanied me to the Vulaines station, under circumstances—night, stillness, and three-part talk—that were unforgettable.

Then comes the announcement of Mallarmé's death ("I found the telegram from Geneviève, 'Father died'") and a description of his burial ("I had barely entered the garden when his daughter threw herself into my arms, weeping and saying: 'Ah! Monsieur V., Papa loved you so much!'"). Valéry is asked to say a few words at the funeral, in the name of the "young people." He chokes again: "I was absolutely unable to utter anything but indistinct mumbles, I was choking and no one understood the four sounds I emitted any better than I did." Then it's all over. Valéry goes home and nurses his illness: "His daughter's last public throes took place, then she was taken away and we left. All that came back to me last night and, as I could no longer breathe, I got up, inhaled some vapor—then a huge storm broke out, and I slept for an hour."

It's all over, but Valéry, whose emotion does not cloud his foresight, goes on writing just long enough to ask Gide not to throw away the letter, which is undeniably superb: "Please keep this letter, which is an accurate description of yesterday. I shall ask you for a copy of it later on, for I have neither the inclination nor the courage to write all this down for myself now." Overwhelmed by grief, having lost the man he loved more than any other, Valéry can still think clearly of his emotion and of what will become of it when he no longer feels it, of what it will mean to him then or *to an other*. It is understandable that he should want to keep a record of such a deep distress. But it is still a little surprising that Valéry is so attached to his letter that—for the first time—he makes a point of asking his correspondent not to lose it. Of all his letters to Gide, this one is most clearly the source of one of his literary texts. His article, "Dernière visite à Mallarmé," which appeared for the first time in 1923 and was reprinted in various collections (including *Variété II*), is based on the first part of the letter and its "accurate description" of 1898. The letter clearly inspires the article, although some of the details are no longer completely accurate (Geneviève, the undershirt, and the perfume disappear, the stroll is moved up to the afternoon, and the drafts of *Hérodiade* are replaced by *Un coup de dés*).

Did Valéry (who had renounced literature) have a poetic ulterior motive in 1898? Was he, before having even made his exit, preparing for his literary comeback (in the 1920s when, flaunting his intimacy with his illustrious elder, he would be acclaimed as Mallarmé's official heir)? Nothing in his correspondence with Gide or elsewhere lets us know for sure. But he certainly would not be the first writer to speculate on the future publication and fame of his letters. (He did contemplate the eventual publication of his notebooks, even while insisting on their private nature.) After all, the publication of writers' (or future writers') letters is no new or strange phenomenon in the history of French literature. Like so many others, Valéry could have been preparing his own autobiographical script, bearing in mind that he might some day become, in spite of himself, an author.

So there is nothing particularly original in Valéry's request to Gide, if it implies only a hint of some literary value to the sincere emotions expressed in the letter. What is interesting is the context in which he makes the request. One does not often have the chance to describe Mallarmé's funeral, and Valéry's involvement in the literary composition of his letter is much greater than usual.[1] The death of his distinguished teacher and literary elder gives his letter enough weight for him to want it saved. In sending it to Gide, Valéry, generally more remote, tries to become one with his words. Having been long under the influence of Mallarmé's fascinating asceticism of the disappearance of the poet as speaker, of the deemphasized "I," Valéry's "I" can at last emerge. With the death of the most perfect of poets, Valéry is now able to come into his own. He is reborn from the ashes of the poet who refused all personal or intimate discourse and can finally express the personal grief of having lost the man who would probably not have wanted to hear the descriptions of such a grief. (Death for Mallarmé? It is "a stream not very deep and slandered.")

When asked to speak at the poet's grave, Valéry chokes. The appropriate, impersonal phrases he is expected to deliver stick in his throat. Only at home, far from the cemetery, after a fumigation and a thunderstorm, can he think of "his" Mallarmé. Words come back to him when only Gide can hear them. They come back to him so well that he thinks of their future: of how time will prove their timelessness. The letter of September 12, 1898, marks a new beginning for Valéry, even though or perhaps because, it is still confidential. Mallarmé's death opens his way to a personal form of literature: a private literature not intended for an audience, which expresses the parts of his self usually reserved for himself. I see in the "Please keep this letter, which is an accurate description of yesterday," a new birth for Valéry—as a writer in search of his unshareable singularity (which eventually finds its home in the *Cahiers*). This rebirth, however, manifests itself through his famous "silence" (which lasts until the publication of *La jeune parque* in 1917). Silence is profoundly necessary at this point: it gives him time to find and understand his deepest, most buried self. He writes henceforth for himself alone—or at least he appears to be writing only for himself (which is, after all, the only real law of private writing). Unable to speak at Mallarmé's grave, Valéry, through his twenty-year silence, buries for the second time the poet for whom language was a public act. In the meantime, he asks his closest confidant to preserve Mallarmé's memory for posterity, for the future when, finally assured of his status as a writer, Valéry will be able to speak of the deceased without choking.

The change in Valéry's life, granted, is not due exclusively to Mallarmé's death, and the letter to Gide is merely symbolic of a greater movement. It indicates the temptation toward personal writing that, although it intensifies after 1898, Valéry had been feeling for several years. Mallarmé's death marks the end, or beginning of the end, of a phase in Valéry's life—especially where Gide is concerned. They continue to correspond until Valéry's death in 1945, but the involvement in the correspondence seems at its peak, on both sides, between 1891 and 1900. For Valéry, the correspondence serves as an outlet for a kind of writing intended for himself alone. The epistolary mode is a kind of paradoxical guarantee of secrecy. It is as if Valéry needs another person to acknowledge the privacy of his writing, to help him hide it from the eyes of the Other (of all others), whom he thinks of with hostile anxiety.[2]

Valéry entrusts the description of Mallarmé's burial to Gide because, since 1891, their correspondence has assumed a strange pact of confidentiality, allowing them to write a kind of secret literature: a literature whose literary qualities will not be acknowledged until later. It is worth noting that the agreement is first proposed explicitly by Gide, quite early in the correspondence:

I should like (even if the only result of this correspondence is your fortunate arrival in Paris)—I should like it to have a certain unity, a certain fixed tone, a certain stable originality, which will give it a very special flavor; finally, I should like to talk with you about things that I cannot talk about with others, and should like you to do the same. For example, as it seems to me you have suggested, each one of these letters would be some subtle landscape of the soul, full of quivering half-tones and delicate analogies awakening like echoes of the vibrations of harmonics;—some specious vision that would be followed, in a gentle flow, by the deductions of our dreams. And this kind of confiding would reveal us one to the other, strangely and delightfully, by showing one of us the association of such fragile images in the other . . . Please tell me, and very quickly— is that what you want—is it? or if it's something else? At any rate, this kind of confiding might be merely one part of our letters and the rest might be filled with some amusing futility—some tale *ad libitum,* some critical daydream about something recently read—we might even, if you absolutely insist, speak of literature. *(January 16, 1891)*

Let us paint the landscapes of our souls for each other, sincerely, without frills or pretension; and if, by chance, we express ourselves well, there is of course no harm done. Their letters become a means of writing poetry in secret, of expressing their confidences with delicate analogies and vibrant harmonics; the letters should work together as a consistent, melodic ensemble, but never, in any circumstances, be referred to as literature (that is for later, when it becomes inevitable and even desirable): "Do please understand that I am not putting under the heading of 'literature' our own productions and our plans and our dreams."

Do not forget to forget literature: this is Gide's epistolary contract. It is, unfortunately, untenable. After a praiseworthy effort at nonliterary reverie ("There were artisans, friends of Death, who polished tombstones, with some *eternal* resignation, at the pale close of a beautiful winter's day. The earth was maternal and made me think of ideal, deep, and solemn graves—graves of souls, at the pale close of a beautiful winter's day" [January 19, 1891]), Valéry returns always to Baudelaire or Poe or to his own poetry, pathetic as it is in his opinion—which does not stop him from showing it to Gide, who can always write it off as a simple "landscape of the soul" or as nothing at all. "Here are a few lines that are not yet written and never will be . . . It is a play of vague words, plus a perfume, not yet music, less than nothing" (February 1891). As for Gide, he gets straight to the point: "In my very first letter I fail to keep my promise: I'm going to speak to you of literature, and do forgive me" (January 26, 1891). His letter continues with admiration for Mallarmé: "it is an enraptured merging of me into him. He has written all the poetry I should have dreamed of writing." Valéry soon echoes this, in almost the same terms: "To have not written that poetry and to write poetry! And this supreme poem oppresses me like a twinge of remorse!" (February 1891). In the shadow of Mallarmé's poetic perfection, poetry is impossible; or, if it is to exist, it must be disguised, converted into confidential reveries—ideas, dreams, perfumes, landscapes of the soul, entrusted to a favorite correspondent, with no responsibility to the reading public.

The correspondence between Gide and Valéry "produces" privacy entirely in the service of literature. Letters become a space apart, a kind of writing workshop or testing ground. It is not surprising that there is no real exchange between them, that what is personal for one is never personal for the other. Although their confidential letters teach them to write, Gide and Valéry never have all that much to say to each other, and their poetic ventures and ideas remain very different. This is perhaps the most striking element of the letters: even the outbursts are theoretical or rhetorical, and the confidentiality pact leads oddly to an extreme reserve on both sides. Gide, at least, reproaches Valéry for his restraint and tries to engage him in a more intimate dialogue:

> I should like to get into your personal life somewhat and to be led there by you yourself. All my efforts to please are meant only for that senti-mental initiation. Tell me, for example, whether you believe that love is bearable—and how; or avoidable—and how; or if it is desirable. But speak to me: I assure you that a few pages of my book will give away to you more than numerous letters would give you away to me. And I am sometimes terrified at thus prostituting my poor virgin soul in the shop windows at every crossroads. *(February 1891)*

He returns to this complaint several times, with varying degrees of insistence: "I cannot be satisfied with an imperfect communion, and your letter is too exquisite not to make me wish for a surrender of your most intimate thoughts: in affection I suffer from all that the other hides from me—from me who can hide nothing" (March 21, 1891). Or, "But your heart and your body are still a mystery to me, and I don't know how to speak to you of yourself, although I know that we will agree on all things" (July 14–15, 1891).

The paradox of their intimacy is that Gide wants Valéry to confide in him more, to write about his feelings, desires, pleasures, the secrets of his heart and body—to write as Gide, poor, prostituted soul, does in his letters and *elsewhere,* publicly, in his books and in the shop windows at every crossroad. Having begun with the intention to confide everything, the two correspondents end in a strange misunder-standing: one of them has no feelings to write about, and the other has already made a full confession to the world. Gide's most intimate desires are inseparable from his writing to such an extent that it seems unnecessary to put in his letters what he has already described at such length in his books. His private life is a kind of ethos that almost all of his written texts already embody. (They are all written to some ex-tent—like his *Journal* or *L'immoraliste* or *La porte étroite*—in the form of a confession, or at least an admission.)

153

By resisting this ethos, Valéry also resists Gide's demands for intimacy. Gide's confessional style has little relation to Valéry's ideas of literature:

> I never divulge my soul in verse or in any other kind of literature (except this kind, which is not literature), for writing! does not mean making one's self blush, or confronting indifference—but rather the ambition, to begin with, of grabbing hold of an ideal reader and unemotionally dragging him off—or of dazzling him, dazing him, conquering him by the higher Truth and the magic, yes, marvelous! force of creating anything one wants with little signs like these! *(September 1891)*

For Valéry writing involves, not a confession or depiction of his desire, which would expose him de facto to the scrutiny of the Other, but an experiment, a mastery of writing as such. He imagines an ideal reader (as opposed to a real or potential reader), who is as similar to him as possible but also unique, a sine qua non if his talent is to be confirmed. Valéry's ideal reader must therefore be someone with whom he is intimate, almost an extension of himself: "Just the idea that *anyone could read what I had written* in secret and with the adventurous feeling of solitude was unbearable to me—Stronger even than physical modesty—A strange feeling, because why write if not for others? Perhaps it was to form and release the other me, the ideal reader who *exists* necessarily in anyone who writes."[3] Hence his interest in an epistolary exchange with a unique confidant, an other with whom he has much in common:

> And I dream of that admirable literature which we might invent: each writing his books entirely for one Person . . . But is that not the magic and fragile virtue of Correspondence? The letter, which forces us to describe the friendly perfume of present minutes, without forgetting the intentions of the night before, when we saw each other, is that not an ornamental and charming work of art, a delight consented to by two and with Time, the true essence of the hour's emotion, and which goes a bit flat in the drawer, just enough to gain in refinement? *(November 16, 1891)*

Gide and Valéry thus have distinctly different reasons for writing to each other. Gide does it to rehearse his own confessions and as a form of seduction, to inspire another's confessions. Intimacy is the chance to reveal himself to another person, and his letters form an intermediate phase between absolute privacy and the full exposure he experiences on publication. Gide's letters are the first drafts of future novels, in which the addressee serves as a stand-in for the general public, an other who represents the Other.[4]

The addressee in Valéry's letters, on the other hand, is an extension of his "I." Valéry must be able to write as if to himself, to hear himself speak without interference and to see himself more clearly through the other's reception of his thoughts. Gide is the closest Valéry can come to the ideal reader—at least he gives the illusion that an ideal reader can exist. As Valéry comments on the adoption of the informal "tu" in their letters:

> First of all we address each other as "tu," which means we speak beyond our time like the great Ancients or early Christians. "Tu" is a free gesture, a pure one. In English, one only addresses God that way: "Thou, God, Thou, Lord!" When you are truly intimate, in the dark, a murmured "tu" gives the illusion of a word addressed to oneself and of an answer from oneself. Doesn't it? (*December 3, 1891*)

For Valéry, the epistolary mode is the most euphoric stage of private writing. It brings his ideal double and reader to life. His "you," armed with a face and an identity, shields him from the vast, faceless Other and its disquieting influence.

For Valéry (and for Gide, to a lesser extent), there is an undeniable continuity between his letter writing and many—in my opinion, the most interesting—aspects of his literary work. His correspondence with Gide gives him the opportunity to experiment and to write, ostensibly, for himself—as he also tries to do in the *Cahiers*, one of the most impressive existing examples of private writing. And this is doubtless why only Gide could predict and plan for Valéry's literary return, by asking him to publish his poems in the newly founded *Nouvelle revue française,* which he and his friends were editing. The difference between the Gide whom Valéry asks to save his letter of September 12, 1898, and the Gide who publishes his friend's *La jeune parque* in 1917 is smaller than it seems. From the start Gide has been the instigator and guardian of the work Valéry refuses to publish. He acknowledges Valéry's refusal and transmits it to the Other. (The Other must know its own limits.) The goal of private writing is perhaps just that: to have one's rejection of the Other eventually exposed and recognized. Valéry, perhaps thanks to Gide, is a writer in spite of himself.

The Intimate Exchange

Reluctant to recognize his writing as a literary endeavor, Valéry finds a refuge in his letters to Gide, at least during the first few years of their correspondence. The epistolary form often provides a last resort for the unwilling or hesitant writer. It also works, on the other hand, as a last resort for those who have tried unsuccessfully to create literature. Rilke, whose innumerable letters depict less of a resistance than an inability to establish himself as a poet, falls into the latter category. While Valéry writes in order to bring his private identity into the open, Rilke can never fully convince himself of the *existence* of his identity, nor can he transcribe it into poetry or give it any kind of literary consistency. Only in letters does his "I" acquire both form and substance.

Rilke—again unlike Valéry—always acknowledges the literary value of his letters, as do many critics and scholars. He often mentions it and even apologizes for letters that are less well-written than usual: "Here you have, my dear Princess, nothing that is really written, just an hour spent over a cup of tea, as it came to my mind, as it had to come . . ." (to Marie von Thurn und Taxis, December 30, 1911). He sometimes has to work to keep them from being too literary, as in one of his first letters to Nanny Wunderly-Volkart: "my correspondence with you should not get the upper hand; with you, I want to ensure that nothing which is part of my work passes into my letters" (December 17, 1919). Rilke promises to try to avoid a confusion of literature with letters—implying that, given the character of his writing, it will require an effort. His prose tends to become literary without his realizing it, or at least despite his best intentions.

In his letters Rilke tries to capture the poetic impulse that evades him in his other writing. He experiments with a kind of writing he feels not fully capable of producing elsewhere. In his important letter to Nanny Wunderly (quoted in the first chapter), Rilke asks himself whether his numerous correspondences function for him as a kind of substitute homeland, whether they give form to a world he cannot otherwise share—for example, with his daughter. A few lines later he seems to abandon this theory (inasmuch as it involves his daughter) in favor of another:

> No, I am not doing it for her; but rather for the "idea," for that which is my work—after all, there is in all letters a trace of its intensity, vibrating and communicating itself; nothing which has once vibrated *beyond* a certain degree of intensity gets lost, and it is true that in my letters I live entirely *above* this degree; only when faced with myself do I fall into inertia, into pure heaviness; alas, no one stands steadfast before his own heart. *(January 14, 1920)*

Another paradox of intimacy: Rilke's poetic experience seems inextricably bound to the need to formulate and reveal his private self, to find himself ("to become his own contemporary again," as he says when he finally finishes the *Elegies*), and perhaps also to the need to situate himself somewhere (in his *Heimat*) that will confirm his existence. As long as the means of fulfilling these needs remain hidden, he finds it impossible to see himself without melting or turning into stone. His interior self, and the object of all his attentions, is decidedly unpresentable, even repulsive, not appropriate company for decent people. Its presence is bearable only for very short periods of time, and perhaps this is the source of Rilke's centrifugal force, the reason for his constant movement *(reiten, reiten . . .)*. The letter to Nanny

Wunderly cited above is clear on this point: the intimate, that vibrant "idea," appears only when words pass from thought toward the exterior, on their journey to another. Rilke's actual travels are merely the metaphor or record in real space of this mental journey. Poetry—or what he refers to simply as his "work"—produces an intensity that is felt, first of all, in the self. But he feels the vibration only fleetingly, when sharing or confiding in others. Hence his incredible involvement in his letters, which end up replacing his other work and substituting as much for his *Heimat* as for the closeness he never manages to achieve with himself. Although his letters do register a certain vibrant intensity, that intimate quality is quickly gone—simply because, in order to appear at all, it must be transmitted to others.

Rilke's letters are like a private diary that he cannot keep to himself. "That was a good long letter, wasn't it? It was almost not a letter, but a little Diary that you will read with indulgence," he writes to Nanny Wunderly (May 16, 1921). The same motif appears in his correspondence with Lou Andreas-Salomé: "I am writing all this down, dear Lou, as if into a diary, being unable to write a letter now and wanting nevertheless to talk to you. I am almost unaccustomed to writing, and you must forgive me therefore if this letter is pitiful and without order" (November 13, 1903). Rilke has so much to do that he has no time left to work or even to write letters. He confides in his correspondents, but he does not really correspond with them. He neither addresses them personally nor asks personal questions. They are mere witnesses to the confessions he makes to himself; they register the ideas that pass through his mind (rather, those that will not simply pass through his mind). This understanding is expressed the most directly in another letter to Nanny Wunderly:

> Dear, I am allowed to say *everything,* you wrote at the end of your letter before the New Year. Now you will see what that *everything* is that can come . . . But all of this should be shown and communicated in such a manner that the other person cannot take it too personally; not as a decision for him, a direction or inclination *towards him,* but only as the

voice of someone who watches, who passes through, not without loving, but still without lingering. *(January 3, 1920)*

Don't imagine that I am speaking *to you*. Be happy just to watch me pass through, or to watch me pass through you, since I can find myself only by confiding in you. This is the most important ethos in Rilke's letters. It is in his letters to Lou that he seems to discover the pleasures of confiding in others. He becomes profoundly addicted. For a long time, Lou seems his only refuge. He writes to her when words escape him elsewhere, when no image or "thing" can emerge from his thoughts. She is the only person with whom he shares the oppressive sterility of his years in Paris: "If I was able to write to you about it, it was because I feel this great need to open myself to you, so that you can comprehend me entirely; but it was only a letter. And so far nothing has been taking shape, or any form which could testify for me: will it ever come?" (July 25, 1903). During a period when his imagination produces nothing tangible and poetry remains out of reach, Rilke finds himself only by sending himself to Lou, by dreaming of flowing into her, and by realizing this dream in letters:

> But I, Lou, your somehow lost son, for a long, long time to come I can be no teller of tales, no soothsayer of my way, no chronicler of my past fortunes; what you hear is only the sound of my steps, continuing, still retreating along uncertain paths, distancing themselves from I don't know what, and whether they are leading me towards anyone I do not know. Only that my mouth, when it has become a great river, may one day flow into you, into your hearing and into the stillnes of your opened depths—that is my prayer, which I recite at every powerful moment, at every moment of dread, longing, or joy, which can preserve and listen. *(January 15, 1904)*

Rilke entrusts Lou with the "I" he cannot define in the hope that it will come back to him, formed and defined by her understanding. Again this pact becomes more or less explicit in the early days of the correspondence: "I can only ask advice from you; only you know who I am. Only you can help me, and I have felt from your very first letter the effect which your calm words have on me. You can explain to me what escapes me, you can tell me what I must do; you know what I need to fear and what I do not: do I have a reason to be afraid? . . . It is you who will know" (June 30, 1903). "Only you know who I am": the epistolary exchange is rarely so similar to a transference, in the psychoanalytical sense of the word. Lou is the guardian of Rilke's inner self; she knows who he is. He confides in her blindly (which takes little effort, considering that he is unable to see himself anyway—imagery is not his forte). She is also the only person he believes in: "my trust in everything you say provides me with assurance and confidence" (August 11, 1903).

Though their relationship resembles one of transference, it never actually becomes one, mostly because of their absolute and threatening closeness. Lou is always a confidante for Rilke, never an analyst. Around 1911 he discusses with Lou (who has become a friend of Freud's and an analyst herself) the possibility of going into analysis, but decides against it: "I am thinking less than before of a doctor. Psychoanalysis is too basic a help for me, it helps once and for all, it clears out, and to find myself cleared out one day would perhaps be even more hopeless than this disorder" (December 28, 1911). An in-depth psychoanalysis, *sie raümt auf,* would make things a little too tidy; it would wash away the personal stamp with which Rilke tries to mark off his own space. It might require him to put an end to his postal confidences, to Lou and to others. It might put an end to his writing in general. In a letter to Lou dated January 20, 1912, Rilke describes the therapeutic aspects of his writing, referring to it as self-treatment *(Selbstbehandlung)* and reiterating his hesitation to undergo psychoanalysis. During the same time period, he begins writing the *Elegies,* as if they were directly inspired by his decision not to go into therapy.[5]

Years later, Rilke's demands on Lou are still the same, except that she can now answer his fiction, *Malte,* written in 1910, as if it were a letter:

You see, I am still in a hurry to get to myself, I still presume that this theme can be of interest; will you involve yourself once more? Please, please, do, I will help you, as best I can, perhaps I'll be bad at it. But there is a point of departure: Malte Laurids Brigge. I need no answers to my books, that you know,—but now I deeply need to know what impression this book made on you. Our good Ellen Key naturally immediately confused me with Malte and gave me up; but no one but you, dear Lou, can distinguish and indicate if and how much he resembles me. *(December 28, 1911)*

Is Malte, the melancholy surveyor of the inhumanity of modern cities, actually Rilke? Only Lou knows. Only Lou knows what Malte means to Rilke and whether he should or should not identify with him. Some people see their letters as literature, others turn their literary texts into letters. *The Notebooks of Malte Laurids Brigge* allow Rilke to continue what his epistolary writing began, the quest for his own identity. The connection is even closer than it may seem. Portions of *Malte* began almost verbatim as letters to Lou. Compare, for example, the Parisian scenes of *Malte* with some of Rilke's letters from 1903 (especially the unusually long one dated July 18).

The relation is symmetrical. The entire first part of *Malte* (set in Paris) is written in the form of a long letter addressed to someone with whom Malte has parted ways, who is now unreachable (almost Lou's shadow): "I am attempting to write to you, although there is really nothing to say after a necessary leave-taking."[6] Rilke's adaptation of *Malte* from a first draft in the form of letters to Lou to its final fictional version also reflects the loss of a "correspondent," the movement toward the intransitive needed to change the book from letter to poem: "My God, if any of it could be shared! But would it *be* then, would it *be*? No, it *is* only at the price of solitude."[7] For something to be shared, it must be addressed to no one. Or such is Malte's theory of reception, and Rilke's: on one hand, he writes to Lou without really involving her personally; on the other, he confides all his texts to her, to her in particular. The last few pages of *Malte* echo this ambiguity. The epistolary form disappears, but it is replaced by a vibrant and symbolic eulogy to the great women letter writers of history, those who have kept the love letter alive: the Portuguese Nun, Heloise, Louise Labbé, Julie de Lespinasse, and so on, all scholars of incommunicability and solitude, as Malte has become.

"And one day I would like to be allowed to come and lay the prayers, the new ones together with the others, at your place, in your hands, in your quiet house. Because, you see, I am a stranger and a poor man, and I am only passing through; but in your hands shall be everything that might have been my home, had I been stronger" (to Lou, July 18, 1903). "In your hands shall be everything": the boundary between letters and work fades when they are addressed to Lou, the audience for all of Rilke's writing. Lou reads his letters and books in the same light. Her responses confirm this. She sees his writing as an ongoing, unified process: "Your letter has arrived, and it is like a supplement to your book on Rodin" (August 10, 1903). His book *Rodin* may be a postscript to one of his letters (he writes repeatedly about Rodin in his letters to Lou) or to all of his previous letters, which Lou judges from a perspective that is more aesthetic than personal.

Her reply to his letter of July 18, 1903, is not without interest in this respect: "While reading your last letter, at times, I forgot you entirely—I was so strongly impressed by your descriptions, so true in their least detail, and yet transcendent enough to acquire a vast human dimension" (July 22, 1903). Her reaction is almost ironic: Rilke writes to Lou in order to be seen by her, to see himself through her eyes, and yet, when reading his letters, she forgets his existence, as she would with any other writer. Is this because he appears first and foremost as a writer even in letters, as a composer of texts addressed to no one in particular, addressed to someone beyond Lou? Almost all the extracts given above suggest this conclusion. In any case, in order to write to her, Rilke needs the same solitude and silence necessary for his poetic work, which he tries to find through his travels and retreats—in Amalfi, for example: "Perhaps I will find there the solitude and great tranquility that everything in me yearns for; then I wish to live quietly, in the company of things, grateful for all that will protect me against the all-too-common. And I wish to write to you from time to time, and tell you more about the things which cannot be discussed now, given the agitation in my existence" (August 1, 1903).

Above all, Lou seems to be the guardian of Rilke's work to come, as Blanchot would call it. She receives not only the preliminary sketches for this work, always too fragmented to keep his attention, but also all the missing texts that prevent him from actually creating his masterpiece. In letter after letter, he entrusts his inadequacies to Lou. He writes to her when unable to find the solitude that will allow him to write for himself. Until he can find himself in his great work, he gathers himself together in Lou. She is his anchor. She counterbalances his constant diffusion and fragmentation. Thanks to her, he never completely loses sight of himself, despite all the ruptures that make up his daily life, and comes back to her before each movement or change:

> Now that I am setting out again for a distant country, I ask you, Lou, for the following: welcome this new book of *Prayers,* add it to the first one, read it and be kind to it. I will still take with me copies of certain poems, because I feel that I will want to read from them from time to time; but I will read these fragments in a different light, knowing that the entire text lies in your hands, in you, my equilibrium—protected, read, and gathered by you. *(August 21, 1903)*

(The book he mentions is, of course, a manuscript.)

He returns to Lou after the fact as well: just after his death, Lou decides to write *Rainer Maria Rilke.* He has spent his life confiding in her so that he can see himself through her eyes, but her portrait of him comes only when he is no longer around to see it. So many letters written for nothing, it would seem. But this is not quite true—Rilke's letters constitute almost half of Lou's book. It is more a self-portrait than a portrait, a self-portrait that, like the rest of Rilke's writing, has passed through Lou. His letters always seem to arrive at their destination sooner or later.

Valéry dreams of being his own and only reader; hence his relative disdain for publication and his interest in an epistolary compromise where he has only one reader, an intimate friend he knows almost as well as he knows himself. But Rilke finds it almost impossible to read himself, to face what he has written. His epistolary exchanges are an attempt to fill the gap left by his nonexistent self-image with another's image of him. The other must be able to see him when he repulses himself, and the relative success of these attempts determines the extent to which Rilke becomes involved in his correspondence. The only correspondents who count for him are those who can see him, who accept the position of intimate reader that Valéry tries to occupy for himself. Rilke's correspondents must be able to read and understand him fully. They must be able to read his texts before they are written, to read the texts that he will never write and the inexpressible things that his epistolary smalltalk hides. "The book will follow, take me at my word, but not literally": this might be the postscript to all Rilke's letters, whose addressees (Lou, Marie, Nanny) are experienced readers of a nonexistent, potential work.

Rilke can only read himself when he is being seen by someone else, through letters and also in person when he finally presents the *Elegies* to his confidantes. On February 11, 1922, he finishes the *Duino Elegies* and rushes to tell Marie von Thurn und Taxis, owner of the Duino estate and guardian for several years of various drafts and outlines of the *Elegies* that she has translated into Italian and sometimes reads to her close friends (with Rilke's permission, although he refuses any wider form of distribution). The most obvious next step would be to send the princess a copy of the new text, but Rilke hesitates and delays. The princess must come to Muzot to hear Rilke read the poems aloud—such is the postscript to Rilke's euphoric letter of February 11: "Please, dear Princess, do not consider it a subterfuge of my laziness when I tell you why I am *not* copying down and sending you the new elegies now: I would be jealous of your reading them. I feel as if it should be *I*, absolutely, who first reads them to you. When? Well, let us hope, soon."

This strange jealousy sums up his epistolary mode as a whole: Rilke wants to be the first to read the *Elegies* to the princess; he wants to read them in her place, to be *her* reading them for the first time. She must come to Muzot where the poems were written so that he can finally hear his own voice through her ears and be reborn as his own reader and contemporary. The actual scene is described a little later, in a letter to Nanny Wunderly (almost as if it had been his only reason for writing the *Elegies*): "Then, the 7th, the day before yesterday, was the big day at Muzot. But I must tell you about it *in person*, my dear. The *way* in which the Princess received the *Elegies* was wonderful (the surroundings and the atmosphere contributed to it), and I must say that I became, with her, a listener and receptor, and that I gave myself a present by reading wonderfully" (June 9, 1922). Rilke would like to tell Nanny the story in person, as an echo of the original scene, the ideal outcome of all his years of writing letters. Rilke's work is definitely not geared toward the disappearance of the poet as speaker. On the contrary, everything in his world (or at least in his world of letters) works toward the poet's appearance. The princess, his faithful correspondent, introduces him to himself by allowing him to read and hear himself. About their second day of reading, devoted to the *Sonnets to Orpheus* (written immediately after the *Elegies*), Rilke later writes: "As for the *Sonnets*, which I took somewhat lightly compared to their older and loftier sisters, the *Elegies*, it was only you, Princess, with your marvellous way of listening to them, who restored them to their full significance for me. Rest assured that your special reception has enriched the already existing work, bringing it to its happy end" (June 14, 1922).

Nanny Wunderly finds herself in a similar position almost two years later, as recipient of a gift whose importance Rilke does not fully acknowledge:

The small packages, alas, aren't a surprise. I thought that you would like
to have, as well as the large and solemnly dedicated edition of the *Elegies,* a small and *intimate* one, which you can easily carry around with
you. I have prepared this edition for you by adding a few verses (half of
them were written last winter, the other half this winter); you will also
find included the original date of each poem; but not only that: I have
read through the entire book, word by word, you cannot read a line
which I haven't already read myself (not to mention the fact that it was
me who wrote all of them . . . Me?). *(December 25, 1923; my italics)*

He gives her a book that is his not because he wrote it but because he
has read it, cover to cover, before sending it to her. He entrusts Nanny
not with his writing, but with his own reading. Nanny has already
read, and even copied out, the *Elegies.* She is now expected to read
his reading of them. As the ideal correspondent, once again, she gives
Rilke the opportunity to see himself.

Mallarmé wanted his work to stand on its own: "Impersonified, the
book, to the same extent as one separates oneself from it as author,
does not demand a reader. Such, between the human accessories, it
exists alone: fact, being."[8] For Rilke's book to exist a reader is imperative—a close friend with a personalized edition, so that the writer will
never again lose himself from sight. And that is all he needs in order
to exist: the reader—a witness, through letters, to the formation and
formulation of the work—is a prerequisite for any work by Rilke, so
necessary in fact that the book itself may have to wait years for its
reader to undergo the proper epistolary preparation. The book exists
only to be read to those long-term correspondents to whom it has
been confided; readers who, to tell the truth, demand the reading
more than the book. Nothing during the last four years of Rilke's life
is ever as fulfilling as the two days in June 1922 spent reading to the
princess. This is the bitter note of his last years: as if neither the *Elegies*
nor the *Sonnets to Orpheus* had ever existed, as if all that had ever
counted were those days in June, in Muzot, where he was able to
become, for the length of a recitation, the man he had spent his life
pursuing in letters.

Forbidden Readers

The status of private or personal writing is often far less clear than it seems. On March 13, 1913, Kafka makes a proposition that has always struck me as strange:

> How would it be, dearest, if instead of letters I were to send you pages of my diary? No matter how little happens, how pointless it may be, how great my indifference to it all, I miss not keeping a diary. But unless you were to read it, it wouldn't be a diary to me. And the changes and omissions necessary in a diary meant for you would surely be all the more beneficial and instructive for me. Do you agree? The difference as compared to my letters will be that the pages of my diary may sometimes contain more substance, but will certainly be even more boring and even more brutal than my letters. But don't be too alarmed; my love for you will not be absent from them.

Kafka writes so many letters to Felice that he has no time left to write in his diary. He misses the chance to write *for himself*, even about trivial things and even when he has nothing to say to himself. Perhaps it is only because he writes so much to Felice that he feels this need. Speaking to her at such length, he finds he can no longer speak to himself; his own speech now comes only when addressed to someone else. Either way, Kafka wastes no time worrying about the ambiguity of his actions. He misses his diary, his private refuge, but at this point it will have meaning only if Felice reads it. Ideally, she should read not the letters intended for her, but the confidences Kafka makes to himself, no matter how boring. (Or at least a censored version of them—he will of course have to change or omit certain parts.) Near the beginning of their relationship, Kafka had proposed to do the same for her—to read a diary she would write for herself instead of letters. He answers Felice's first letter with this comment: "Please write me another [letter] soon. Don't make an effort, a letter requires effort, however one looks at it; just keep a little diary for me; this demands less and gives more. Of course you will have to write more in it than you would for yourself alone, since I don't really know you at all" (September 28, 1912).

The transformation of letters into a diary, or the editing of a diary into sections to be mailed daily to someone else (no longer really a correspondent): in a way, Kafka's desires are similar to Rilke's, for whom the two genres (all genres, perhaps) are more or less identical. For both men, the difference between writing for a correspondent and writing for oneself is minimal enough to allow for various substitutions and ambiguities. But in Kafka's case the distinction never completely disappears, and his writing is very different from Rilke's. Realizing that the two genres are so close, he makes a conscious effort to avoid confusing them. Four days after his proposition to Felice, he hesitates: "I haven't the heart to write the diary after all, Felice . . . Inevitably it would be full of unbearable things, quite impossible things, and would you really be capable, dearest, of reading the pages simply as a diary, and not as a letter? I would have to have this assurance in advance" (March 17–18, 1913).

Although the content of his journal and his letters may be alike, the two could not be read in the same way. Kafka hesitates to send his journal because he is not quite sure that Felice is capable of making the distinction. It is an insoluble problem: how to prevent Felice from mistaking these pages, which are not addressed to her but which she must read (their existence depends on it), for a letter? How to prevent her from believing that his writing is addressed to her, when it arrives through the mail? He might as well ask her not to mistake herself for Felice Bauer.

But that is exactly what he asks her to do: not to be herself, to detach herself from herself, to become the impersonal reader of works not intended *for* her, even if sent *to* her. Unlike Rilke's letters, Kafka's never resolve the conflict between addressee and recipient (to use Albert Rombaud's distinction[9]), between the anonymous reader for whom he writes and the identified reader to whom he writes. Kafka needs a receptor for his letters, but only in order to call her existence into question by making her the addressee of his works. Two days after having sent his first letter to Felice, Kafka writes "The Judgment" in one night and dedicates it to his correspondent, evidently without her knowledge. He waits a month to tell her, after the correspondence is off the ground and it is too late to change the dedication: "This spring, at the latest, Rowohlt of Leipzig will publish a *Yearbook of Poetry,* edited by Max. It will include one of my short stories, 'The Judgment,' which will be dedicated 'To Fräulein Felice B.' Is this dealing too imperiously with your rights? The more so since this dedication was written a month ago, and the manuscript is no longer in my possession?" (October 24, 1912).

Rilke needs to address someone in order to hear or read himself. Kafka needs no one, and no one in particular. Rilke makes use of the anticipated or promised work, Kafka of the fait accompli: "The Judgment" is dedicated to Felice without her consent, almost against her will. It is a text she is not likely to understand, especially since Kafka makes no effort to ensure that she does: "The 'Judgment' cannot be explained. Perhaps one day I'll show you some entries in my diary about it. The story is full of abstractions, though they are never admitted" (June 10, 1913). In order to understand it, she would have to read Kafka's diary, but he decides not to send it to her (she would mistake it for a letter). "The Judgment" may be dedicated to Felice, but it is certainly not addressed to her. It has nothing to do with her: "Besides, so far as I can see, the substance of the story has not the remotest connection with you" (October 24, 1912).

Nothing is more important for Rilke than the presence of a recipient whose understanding of his work affects his own. Kafka, on the contrary, needs Felice's absence, and even her lack of understanding, in order to read *publicly* the work he has dedicated to her (the work he perhaps had to dedicate to her before he could write it and read it publicly). The greater her absence from his life, the greater her presence in his reading: "I enclose an invitation to a reading. I shall be reading your short story ["The Judgment"]. Believe me, you will be there, even if you stay in Berlin. To appear in public with your story, and thus as it were with you, will be a strange feeling. The story is sad and painful, and no one will be able to explain my happy face during the reading" (November 30, 1912).

Reading "The Judgment" aloud, with Felice in Berlin, is a means of presenting himself to an audience with her. She is the woman he has chosen to represent the absence to which his work is devoted. The story is sad, painful, repulsive (enough to prevent Felice from coming to Prague), but Kafka will seem happy when reading it. He will smile—which he is unable to do when he actually sees her or when he poses with her for a photograph (in July 1917, for example—in the picture, he is awkward, one hand curled in on itself as if unwilling to touch her). Felice is not allowed to visit Prague where her suitor gives public readings: Her absence never seems quite so clearly the price Kafka pays for the emergence of his literature as it does in this strange invitation.

Felice thus plays at least two roles in Kafka's life, which is definitely one too many. She is both the recipient of his letters and the ghostly addressee of his literary writing: enough to make her dizzy, considering that at any given time she is always in the wrong role. When he writes to her, it is to let her know that their correspondence takes up too much of his time, and he would rather be writing a diary or a story or a novel that he could address to her: "This is not the only reason why I am going to write only short letters from now on (on Sundays, however, I shall always allow myself the luxury of an enormous letter), but also because I want to spend every ounce of myself on my novel, which after all belongs to you as well, or rather it should give you a clearer idea of the good in me than the mere hints in the longest letters of the longest lifetime" (November 11, 1912).

He writes her a letter to say that he would rather address his fiction to her. He might as well ask her not to move, to remain silent, to disappear, as he does, spending every ounce of himself on the characters he would follow to the underworld if they led him there. Felice must play the role of a benevolent third party who never comes between him and the partners he invents when she is not around:

Dearest, whatever happens I implore you, with hands raised in supplication, not to be jealous of my novel. If the people in my novel get wind of your jealousy, they will run away from me; as it is, I am holding on to them only by the ends of their sleeves. And imagine, if they run away from me I shall have to run after them, even as far as the underworld, where of course they really are at home. *(January 2–3, 1913)*

She must accept these children of the Idumaen night, conceived behind her back, sent to her in place of the children he will never conceive with her (his refusal to have a child, unlike marriage, was never in the least ambiguous): "Today I am sending you the *Stoker*. Receive the little lad kindly, sit him down beside you and praise him, as he longs for you to do" (June 10, 1913).

Inversely, when Kafka works on his fiction, he cannot stop thinking of Felice. He wishes he were writing to her instead, if only for the kindness she, unlike his novel, would show him: "Ah dearest, how lucky I am that now—having barely managed to get through a passage in the novel, a passage with which I don't feel quite at home (the novel still won't obey me, I hold on to it, but it resists me unawares, and I keep having to let it go for whole passages on end)—I am allowed to write to you, who are so very much kinder to me than my novel" (December 12–13, 1912).

The conflict between her roles as recipient of his letters and addressee of his fiction is never truly resolved. And perhaps it is not intended to be. Kafka seems able to write only when the identity of his reader is ambiguous. The letter and the novel are two sides of the same coin: when Kafka intends to correspond with Felice, he ends up writing *Amerika* for her, or for her absence. When he sits down to write *Amerika*, Felice emerges from his subconscious, as if the novel were simply a repression or transference of his letter-writing energy—or, to put it into Kafka's words one last time, as if fiction springs from his suppressed epistolary desire: "My dearest girl, all the writing I did today on my novel was nothing but a suppressed desire to write to you, and now I have been punished on both sides; what I wrote is pretty poor . . . and toward you, dearest, it has made me disgruntled and altogether unworthy" (December 17–18, 1912).

Kafka perfects the art of loss, on one level or on both. His fiction emerges somewhere between the writing he cannot produce and the letters he should not produce.

On August 9, 1846, five days after their first night together, Flaubert describes his literary plans to Louise Colet: "Some day, if I write my memoirs—the only thing I shall write well, if ever I settle down to it—you will have a place in them, and what a place! For you are making a wide breach in my existence." If he ever writes his memoirs, Louise will occupy an important place in them, but he never does get around to writing them. Other than certain early works, *Mémoires d'un fou* or *Novembre,* Flaubert systematically refuses to write in the personal vein. Similarly, the role that Louise actually plays in his writing is not too obvious. His memoirs are reserved for her, but since he never writes them she never really appears in his writing. One might almost believe that Flaubert writes in order to exclude Louise from his life, or to forget the memoirs that would include her.

Flaubert, even more than Kafka, takes special care not to confuse his personal writing, tied to particular people, with his true literary writing. But, like Kafka, he uses letters, a private form of writing, to experiment with confusion and absence. Louise's mistake is to believe that her lover's books are addressed to her. Then again, her role is exactly that—to be mistaken, to be twisted and tricked by the *Madame Bovary* she waits in vain to hear during Flaubert's trips to Paris. Judging by Flaubert's regret at having read one of his earlier texts to Louise, he is more or less immune to Rilke's syndrome. He shows this clearly enough when referring to a fragment of the first *Education sentimentale* that he has sent to Louise: "You ask me whether the few lines I sent you were written for you; you would like to know for whom; you are jealous. For no one—like everything I have written. I have always forbidden myself ever to put anything of myself into my works, and yet I have put in a great deal. I have always tried not to make Art subservient to the gratification of any particular person" (August 14–15, 1846).

As all of Flaubert's letters assert in one way or another, he writes for no one, especially not for Louise. His writing is so singular that it is no longer a form of communication: "I write for myself, for myself alone as I smoke and as I sleep.—It's so personal and intimate it's almost an animal function" (August 16, 1847). Flaubert's writing is too intimate, too personal, to be shared with his correspondent, who might suspect that she had played a role in its production, when its very existence depends on the fact that it was written for no one— almost *by* no one. Here the intimate meets the impersonal to form the outer limits of a personal epistolary discourse (addressed to a woman who cannot distinguish between personal letters and impersonal art). Louise is mistaken even in complimenting Flaubert on his letter-writing style, since it is exactly that epistolary tone he is trying to lose. Letters are not his literary goal, nor is she his desired audience: "My letters sometimes amaze you, you say. You find them so well written. Beautiful malice! There, I write what I think. But to think for others as they would think, to make them speak, what a difference!" (September 30, 1853). Letter writing is facile and sterile, the figurehead of personal art, and not even Voltaire's letters can escape this criticism: "People go into raptures over Voltaire's correspondence. But it was the *only* thing the great man was ever capable of! *exposing his personal opinion,* that is; everything he did or wrote came down to that. He was pitiful at theater, at pure poetry" (August 26, 1853).

Flaubert's aesthetic necessarily dismisses the epistolary art. Never do his letters serve any literary purpose, as they do for Rilke. On the contrary, they distract him from his real work. Then why does he write so many? Why take such care with epistolary style, why use it to express his moods and opinions so clearly when he is trying to get rid of them? Because, in order to get rid of them, he must deposit them somewhere else, with someone else. You cannot lose your personality if you keep it to yourself: this is the core of Flaubert's correspondence with Louise Colet. To become impersonal, the invisible god he dreams of being in every sentence he writes,[10] he entrusts his personality to Louise, in letter after letter. Louise takes over the subjectivity that Flaubert must sacrifice (unlike Rilke, who tries desperately to hold on to his).

The "I" in Flaubert's letters is triumphant. If they really constitute a "preface to the writer's life" (to quote the evocative title of the edition of Flaubert's correspondence edited by Geneviève Bollème, two-thirds of which is taken up by the letters to Louise), it is not because they make up the most authentic portrait of the artist. It is because, in them, Flaubert gradually renounces his own personality and its relation to the living (with his permanent mourning). He must decrease so that his work may increase, and for him to decrease, short of cutting his own head off, he must slice himself and his subjectivity into hundreds of letter-sized pieces—the way that others do in poems. Louise will figure it out, because she deals in subjectivity. She in turn is constantly slicing her least moods into verse, in keeping with the fashion of the time. Flaubert fiercely criticizes her for this: "You have turned art into a sewer of passions, a kind of chamber pot into which some unspeakable overflow has been poured.—It does not smell good. It smells of hatred" (January 9–10, 1854). Why would he hesitate to use as a chamber pot the woman who turns art into a sewer?

Flaubert never writes his memoirs because he has already written them, little by little in his letters to Louise: "I have initiated you into my past, into the loves of my youth, into my family and, even more extraordinarily for me, into my work. *You could write my entire story*" (February 27, 1847; my italics). Louise is the archive for Flaubert's autobiography. She could write his memoirs for him, and, in fact, she does not miss the chance: chamber pots must be emptied and they never smell good. Her lover never reads her one line of *Madame Bovary* (although she sends him all of her poems). What he gives her instead is his personality, to do with as she wishes. In 1846 Flaubert talks to Louise about writing his memoirs. Seven years later (a year before their relationship ends), his intentions are very different: "I have really *summed myself up* here and this is the conclusion of these four idle weeks: goodbye, that is goodbye forever to the *personal,* to the private, to the relative. The old plan I had to write my memoirs is gone. Nothing related to myself interests me" (August 26, 1853). A farewell letter to the personal and also probably to Louise, whose relevance to the writer Flaubert is becoming is rapidly decreasing. In the same letter he says: "Yes, I am beginning to be rid of myself and my memories"—"thanks to you," he could have added. Once rid of himself and his memories, Flaubert can finally become a pure projective force. Relieved of his own personality, he can assume all personalities and identify with anyone and everyone. It is not by chance that, in the same letter, he speaks of the desire for metamorphosis: "I am consumed now by the need for metamorphosis. I would like to transcribe all that I see, not as it is, but transfigured . . . The things that I have felt the most come to me transposed to other countries and felt by other people. I change their houses, their costumes, the weather, etc."

Where the letter writer begins to tire of himself and his partner, the novelist appears. One year earlier, however, Flaubert, still working on *Madame Bovary,* wrote to Louise: "I have, thus, during the breaks I take from work, your beautiful and good face before me like a time of rest. Our love is, in this way, a kind of bookmark I place between the pages ahead and that I dream of reaching in every way" (November 22, 1852). The domains of novel and letter overlap, as they do for Kafka. Louise has a place between the unwritten pages of *Madame Bovary,* on the distant horizon; she is waiting there to hear the novel when it is finished. But the horizon is constantly moving, always just as far away, always in the distance. Tomorrow never comes. There is the same discontinuity between letter and novel in Flaubert's work as in Kafka's. When he finally reaches the horizon (Paris) with Emma in his pocket, Louise, the reader he planned to caress with his voice, is gone. He can reach the horizon only when there is no one there to expect him. And perhaps this is the desired return on his epistolary investment.

Exits

Letters serve many functions. For Valéry, they form a kind of shield against an anonymous, numerous audience. With letters he can follow a regime of private writing that helps him not to lose sight of himself. His assumption that there is an undeniable *continuity* between letters and literature places him, paradoxically, in the same camp as Rilke, who uses letters as a release when poetry escapes him (taking his identity with it). For both writers, the literary content of their correspondence, as well as the care they take to ensure that their letters do not get lost, blurs the distinction between the two genres. Both modes of writing are essentially a private activity (at least originally so). If all it took to be a poet were to address yourself to one reader, whom you knew almost as well as you knew yourself, Valéry and Rilke would have been the happiest writers in the world.

Writers like Kafka and Flaubert or Proust and Baudelaire count on an essential *discontinuity* between letters and literature. Their literary texts are written behind the other's back, addressed to no one in particular or to everyone (except those in charge of receiving the letters).[11] They use their letters as a means of *consuming* their correspondents. Valéry and Rilke, on the other hand, use letters as an opening into writing, a kind of workshop where the results of their experiments determine their fate as writers (at least that is what I have tried to show in this book). The literary work is the letter's subtext. Denied or desired, possible or impossible, it is always there, like a belief that each writer manifests in his own way. In the worst-case scenario, the letters end up substituting for it. The private, the personal, and the confidential function as poles of attraction or repulsion; and what they attract or repel forms the foundation of the book, or the Book, conceived by Hegel and the romantics as the ultimate and total work of knowledge and meaning, a book all writers try to shape.

Yet it can happen, as with Mallarmé, that the letter's subtext is not the creation of a literary work, but its destruction. Letters are no longer the preparation for literature but a means of abolishing, or at least of questioning, one's belief in it. Without that belief, the work will never come into being: in Mallarmé's letters, the writer is remarkably absent. Instead of projecting a subject along the straight line toward becoming a writer, they keep him moving and circulating beyond literature. No writer's identity comes to life in the letters, and no literary work is envisioned. The horizon other writers strive to reach is the starting point that Mallarmé leaves behind. Instead of the claim "I write letters in order to become a writer" (with Valéry's and Rilke's variations, "I write letters because I'm not sure I want to be a writer, or because I'm unable to be one"), Mallarmé asserts, "I write letters in order to lose my identity as a writer and my belief in poetry as a salutation."

Between his crayfish, his handshakes, and the gossip he circulates, what is left of his identity? Almost nothing, and it is this absence that Mallarmé the writer must manage: he has to become no one, with his letters to testify to his absence and to give symbolic weight to his position. He takes Flaubert's impulse to a strange extreme—as if, having first lost his personality, he writes to others to resign from the position of writer that others still expect him to occupy. Is Mallarmé a poet? He will not answer the question, and it is no longer his place to answer it. The ideal for Mallarmé would be to talk so much of and for others that he could fall silent about himself and let others write or speak for him. Let his name be murmured here and there, often if necessary, until he himself becomes a "he" to others, a nonperson.

This wish is ironically realized in some of the choices made by the editors of his letters. The collections of his correspondence (especially the later volumes) are among few that I know of to include not only the available letters, but also the lost letters. Others' responses to letters that have not been found are frequently printed (while the responses to letters that have been found are not included). Almost a third of the letters itemized during the last years of his life are "ghost letters": numbered, dated, and classified like the existing letters but with the responses filed in their place. The postal service has its amusements, and so do editors: in Mallarmé's case, even lost letters arrive at their destination. His editors acknowledge the receipt of what was perhaps his most secret desire—to become impersonal to the point of losing his voice entirely to others, to have his letters written by other people. Never is Mallarmé's long silence so telling.

In any case, I can imagine Mallarmé appreciating his editors' choices for what they are (posthumously, of course—he never wished to be, like Rilke, his own contemporary and did all he could to live in the past). After all, exactly the same kind of choice is required by his infamous Book, whose existence depends on its not existing, or existing only in rumors other people have spread, like something imagined or dreamed, written by no one—least of all Mallarmé. If one person were the "I" of the Book, it would become only a book. Necessarily condemned to nonexistence, it represents the end of literature, in the same way that Mallarmé's ghost letters signal the end of his correspondence.

Perhaps the connection between the two is even more fundamental. Perhaps Mallarmé's correspondence, with its silences and missing letters, *is* the Book, or at least one of its chapters. In a famous letter to Verlaine (collected in the *Oeuvres* under the—unconsciously ironic?—heading "Autobiographie"), Mallarmé suggests his plan for the Book:

> What was it? That's hard to say: a book, quite simply, in many volumes, a book which really would be a book, architectural and premeditated, and not an anthology of random inspirations, however marvelous . . . I'll go further and say: the Book, persuaded that when all's said and done there is only one, attempted unwittingly by whoever has written, even those of genius . . . There you have the confession of my vice, laid

bare, dear friend, which a thousand times I've rejected when my spirit was bruised or weary, but it possesses me and I shall perhaps succeed. Not in creating this work in its entirety (you'd have to be I don't know who for that!) but in showing a fragment which had been created, and in making glorious authenticity shine in one place, and in indicating in all its entirety, the rest, which would demand more than one lifetime. To prove by the portions created that this book does exist, and that I've known what I was unable to accomplish. *(November 16, 1885)*

The Book is out of everyone's reach. Its author cannot be limited to one identity or one life. But, at the same time, everyone takes part in its production, everyone believes in it and tries to give it form: "This work exists, everyone has attempted it without knowing it. To show this and lift a corner of the veil from what could be the equivalent poem, is in isolation my pleasure and my torture" (to Vittorio Pica, before November 27, 1886). By definition the Book, like so many of Mallarmé's letters, is written by others and that is the art and challenge of the work—to make others write it. At least, the few fragments of the Book published by J. Scherer suggest this. In them Mallarmé plans to coordinate a ritual or recitation performed by various participants who are unknown to each other and unaware of the project as a whole.

None of the participants can be aware of their role in the production of the Book. Only Mallarmé can follow it, and even he has stopped believing in it. At least he never gets to the point of working on it. He talks about it for years, announces plans to make it, but eventually he is content just to allude to it. The Book is not supposed to be written, it is supposed to be discussed, sometimes in hyperbolic terms: "Since I'm too ambitious, it's not just one genre that I want to affect but all those which, in my view, impinge on the stage: magic, popular, and lyrical dramas. And it's only when I've completed this triple task that I'll present all three almost simultaneously, setting fire, like Nero, to three corners of Paris" (to Mrs. Sarah Helen Whitman, May 18 and 28, 1877). Mallarmé frequently makes this kind of declaration, announcing his impossible plans for an impossible work: to-morrow, soon, I will set Paris on fire and, believe me, it will be a beautiful sight. Years pass and the pyromaniac-poet does not perform. He slides imperceptibly from "Believe me, it will be a beautiful sight" to "Believe me, it would have been a beautiful sight." The Book will never exist, and the only thing left to burn, in the end, are Mallarmé's abandoned papers, which some see as sketches for the Book.[12] Between his first fit of breathlessness and the second one, which will kill him, Mallarmé has just enough time to scrawl out the following: "Recommendation for my papers. Burn them: there is no literary legacy, my poor children . . . Don't even submit them for evaluation: refuse all curious or friendly interference. Say that there is nothing to be seen in them, which is true anyway . . ."

His last letter orders the burning of the outline for his impossible Book, which was to set fire to Paris. It is a useless recommendation, of course: not only because Valéry and others after him will rush to read and then to publish the lack of "literary legacy" Mallarmé left behind, but also because when there is nothing left, there is nothing left to burn. Mallarmé himself has long since set fire, not to Paris, but to the Book and to the belief in the Book as an absolute. Nero and his fires were yesterday, lit one by one as the Prince of Poets dismissed everyone attracted by the idea of the Book—sending writer after writer back to their own writing and their own faith in literature. He sent away not only the one future Academician, greedier for a literary legacy than he seemed at first, but the habitués of the Tuesday salon as well as all of his correspondents. And later, of course, he sent away all of his readers in search of lost meaning, leaving them only their own resources with which to understand his work.

Everyone can participate in the production of the Book: perhaps this is Mallarmé's way of saying that everyone can play a role in maintaining the belief in its possibility (since the Book exists only as an object of faith)—especially the regulars at his Tuesday nights, held primarily for that purpose. The Book's home is 89 rue de Rome: there the "mardistes" celebrate its future publication (just as one celebrates an imminent revolution), without realizing that it exists only in the form of this celebration. If you believe in the Book, visit Mallarmé on Tuesday: "I have so much to do and, although I am now relatively old, and all I have really carried out of my dream is a gesture here and there to listeners" (to Jules Boissière, November 24, 1892). (An editor's note specifies that Mallarmé is speaking here of the allusions he has made to the Book on Tuesday evenings.) If you believe that Mallarmé knows the secret of poetic creation, you are wrong, but come on Tuesday anyway: "Alas, no! dear sir, the only mysteries I hide are those immanent ones that everyone hoards and gives out according to the course of circumstance; but come and join several friends one Tuesday evening, we talk at length and just to see each other, you are right, is not without interest" (to Maurice Pujo, November 24, 1892).[13]

If you believe in the Book, write to Mallarmé: he will maintain your belief, always ready to respond to your least attempt at writing with consistent kindness. *Keep in touch:* he has understood you, he is following your work. The Book is no more than a question sent to Mallarmé. It is an address: 89 rue de Rome. It is formed with everyone's participation and with no one's knowledge: with his friends' visits, their letters, the poems and books they send—more and more numerous as the years go by—which Mallarmé answers with exquisite politeness.[14] The Book is a compilation of papers, with Mallarmé as the secretary-archivist; he files, orders, and arranges the fragments of a work-in-progress formed somewhere between him and his correspondents, in the knowledge that others expect him to have (he is the object of their transference). What he receives is a complete work because it is created by all the others, or at least by their belief in it; a complete work that has retreated and disappeared into his letters, a work that he has been mourning for years.

Mallarmé's correspondence is based on an act of destruction, a dissolution of literature through lack of faith. But literature can also collapse under the weight of too much faith. Mallarmé's path unexpectedly meets up with Artaud's trail. In both cases, the final route to writing is through letters. One writes letters to block off poetic language and the other because his existence depends on its concrete and measurable reception, because he wants his words taken *literally*.

From the moment he appears on the literary scene, through his correspondence with Rivière, Artaud expects to be taken literally, even within the confines of an exchange not designed for that purpose. The ambiguity of his position comes from the fact that he uses literature to bring about decidedly nonliterary ends. He entrusts his unique case, his disease (to use his own term), to literature rather than to medicine or psychoanalysis. He chooses epistolary transference over the therapeutic forms—with the editor of the *Nouvelle revue française* as object of this transference. This is, I believe, the origin of Artaud's madness and the only element we can discuss, having only his texts to read. Artaud's madness is closely tied to literature and uses literary discourse as an outlet for his singular reality.[15] In order to be taken literally, he makes literature authentic, and letters become its most fundamental and permanent form.

This voluntary recycling of literature appears clearly in the exchange with Rivière. When proposing the publication of their letters, Rivière suggests a few adjustments: "There would be only a little work of transposition to be done. I mean that we would give the addressee and the writer fictitious names. Perhaps I could draft a reply based on the one that I sent you, but more developed and less personal. Perhaps we could also include a bit of your poetry or of your essay on Uccello? The whole would make up a little epistolary novel which would be rather unusual" (May 24, 1924). Artaud answers by return mail, refusing any change whatsoever:

> Why lie, why try to put on a literary level something which is the cry of life itself, why give an appearance of fiction to that which is made of the ineradicable substance of the soul, which is like the wail of reality? Yes, your idea pleases me, it delights me, it overwhelms me, but only provided we give the reader the impression that he is not involved with

something fabricated. We have the right to lie, but not about the essence of the thing. I do not insist on signing the letters with my name. But it is absolutely necessary for the reader to feel that he has in his hands the elements of a true story. We would have to publish my letters from the first to the last and to do this we would have to go back to June 1923. *(May 25, 1924)*

Artaud's letters are written outside the realms of fiction and metaphor. They are a "cry of life," the "substance of the soul," written in the most authentic words possible, with the most straightforward meaning possible. There is nothing figurative about them, not the slightest difference between what they say and what they mean. They are, in a way, the ultimate autobiography.

Artaud's protest against fiction begins with his correspondence with Rivière and never ends. In Rodez it becomes more and more extreme, as his first letter to Henri Parisot shows: "I told you to publish *Voyage au pays des Tarahumaras,* and I have written you a letter to be published in place of the supplement which I sent you in 1943. All this is very well but, dear friend, we still cannot rest. There is something else at the moment on earth and in Paris besides literature, publishing, and magazines. There is an old matter which everyone is talking about" (September 17, 1945). In the same letter Artaud writes: "All this is my own personal affair and does not interest you, I sense it, for people read the memoirs of dead poets but while they are alive no one would give them a cup of coffee or a glass of opium to console them." I write so that the world will take me literally, answer me, give me a cup of coffee, or some opium, or whatever, the right to life, to speech, to living speech—and not so that I will be desired or read as literature, hiding behind fiction and metaphor. The disappearance of the poet is not my speciality. How can I disappear when all my attempts to *appear* fail? Artaud's disagreement with his correspondents over the virtues of literature continues, and if Rivière is no longer there to register it, Paulhan and others will: "You have asked me for a book and I take advantage of the request to write you a letter. I don't know whether it will be long because I have only just begun it, but I hope that it will be published since I write it like a poem that is dedicated to you" (September 10, 1945).

He is asked for a book, a work; he answers with a letter, an open letter, which must be published: it is his only poem. It is not literature, even if it becomes in the end more than forty volumes in the hands of a famous Parisian publisher. Nothing is more literary than Artaud's obstinate refusal to write literature. Nothing is more fascinating than the disappearance of literature behind words taken literally, or writing that fathers a real subject, a person. "Literature works toward its own disappearance," wrote Blanchot. Artaud, with his rejection of metaphor, becomes the ultimate metaphor and symbol of this disappearance. He untiringly reinvents his origin, his genealogy, and a language that he does not owe to the Other. And his editors, just as untiringly, publish him, giving form to the moment when, in Blanchot's words, "the work coincides with its own absence." His least declaration, his least sketch or jotting, is published and becomes one more testimonial to the absence of the work, to the existence of this absence.

Artaud becomes a literary monument because everything he writes testifies to a fundamental misunderstanding of the power of literary discourse. This is his madness, or at least his epistolary madness. In a time when readers and writers have been tirelessly analyzing the origin of writing and its inspiration, nothing is more glorious than this kind of fundamental error. It inspires a belief in all that is *only* literature, an error that gives a terribly real weight to the oldest desires of writing. "Languages are imperfect in that although there are many, the supreme one is lacking," wrote Mallarmé, without really complaining, since the absence of an ultimate language to some extent justifies poetry: "philosophically, verse makes up for what languages lack, completely superior as it is." In the place of Mallarmé's remunerative lines, Artaud uses glossolalia, the remnants of a supreme language that the Other has hidden from him. Instead of planning for the Book, a lost object or pure object of belief, he repeatedly accuses the Other of having stolen it from him. Instead of writing around nothing, around the shadows of desire, he demands everything and complains that he can no longer have it. The difference between Artaud's letters and poetry is therefore minimal (both are used to indicate an absence or loss), but absolute. It is the difference between "There is something I cannot say," which Mallarmé's letters echo, and "There is something I am being prevented from saying," which abolishes Artaud's distance from the Book, pushes him across the entire literary space without his ever having entered it. Although letters are used in each case, Mallarmé and Artaud make their exit from literature through the same door used by Kafka, Rilke, Flaubert, and Valéry to come into it. This will be the somewhat terse conclusion to my book: letters are equivocal, either an entrance into literature or an exit out. Each letter writer must find his own door, as *The Trial*'s gatekeeper of the law might say. But that would not stop him from checking all the locks.

Notes

The translator has used standard English translations wherever possible. The following editions are cited:

Antonin Artaud, *Selected Writings,* ed. Susan Sontag, trans. Helen Weaver (New York: Farrar, Straus and Giroux, 1976).
—— *Oeuvres complètes,* 11 vols. (Paris: Gallimard, 1970 1971).
Charles Baudelaire. *Letters to His Mother, 1833–1866,* trans. Arthur Symons (London: John Rodker, 1928).
—— *Letters from His Youth,* trans. Simona Morini and Frederic Tuten (New York: Doubleday, 1970).
—— *Selected Letters: The Conquest of Solitude,* trans. and ed. Rosemary Lloyd (Chicago: University of Chicago Press, 1986).
—— *Correspondance,* vols. 1 and 2, ed. C. Pichois and J. Ziegler (Paris: Bibliothèque de la Pléiade, Gallimard, 1973).
Gustave Flaubert, *Letters, 1830–1857,* ed. and trans. Francis Steegmuller (Cambridge: Harvard University Press, 1980).
—— *Correspondance,* 9 vols. (Paris: Editions Conard, 1926–1933).
—— *Correspondance,* vols. 1 and 2, ed. J. Bruneau (Paris: Bibliothèque de la Pléiade, Gallimard, 1973, 1980).
André Gide and Paul Valéry, *Self-Portraits: The Gide/Valéry Letters, 1890–1942,* ed. Robert Mallet, trans. June Guicharnaud (Chicago: University of Chicago Press, 1966).
—— *Correspondance,* ed. R. Mallet (Paris: Gallimard, 1955).
Franz Kafka, *The Diaries, 1910–1923,* ed. Max Brod (New York: Schocken Books, 1975).
—— *Letters to Felice,* ed. Erich Heller and Jürgen Born, trans. James Stern and Elisabeth Duckworth (New York: Schocken Books, 1973).
—— *Letters to Friends, Family, and Editors,* trans. Richard and Clara Winston (New York: Schocken Books, 1977).

——— *Letters to Milena,* trans. Philip Boehm (New York: Schocken Books, 1990).

Stéphane Mallarmé, *Selected Letters,* ed. and trans. Rosemary Lloyd (Chicago: University of Chicago Press, 1988).

——— *Correspondance,* vol. 1, ed. H. Mondor and J. P. Richard, vols. 2–11, ed. H. Mondor and L. J. Austin (Paris: Gallimard, 1956–1985).

Marcel Proust, *Letters to His Mother,* ed. and trans. George D. Painter (New York: Citadel Press, 1957).

——— *Selected Letters, 1880–1903,* ed. Philip Kolb, trans. Ralph Manheim (Chicago: University of Chicago Press, 1983).

——— *Selected Letters, 1904–1909,* ed. Philip Kolb, trans. Terence Kilmartin (New York: Oxford University Press, 1989).

——— *Correspondance,* ed. Philip Kolb (Paris: Plon, 1970–1988).

Rainer Maria Rilke, *Letters, 1910–1926,* trans. Jane Bannard Greene and M. D. Herter Norton (New York: Norton, 1972).

——— *Letters to Merline, 1919–1922,* trans. Jesse Browner (New York: Paragon House, 1989).

——— and Merline, *Correspondance, 1920–1926* (Zurich: Niehans, 1954).

——— and Lou Andreas-Salomé, *Briefwechsel* (Frankfurt am Main: Insel Verlag, 1975).

——— *Briefe an Nanny Wunderly-Volkart,* vols. 1 and 2 (Frankfurt am Main: Insel Verlag, 1975).

Introduction: Reading in Bed

1. Jacques Lacan, "La direction de la cure," *Ecrits* (Paris: Editions du Seuil, 1966), p. 589.
2. I am thinking specifically of the works of the Ecole de Constance, most notably those of H.-R. Jauss and W. Iser.
3. See Maurice Blanchot, *L'espace littéraire* (Paris: Gallimard, 1955), and *Le livre à venir* (Paris: Gallimard, 1959).
4. Stéphane Mallarmé, *Selected Poetry and Prose,* ed. Mary Ann Caws (New York: New Directions, 1982), p. 75.
5. Jean Paulhan and Francis Ponge, *Correspondance, 1923–1968;* vol. 1, 1923–1946 (Paris: Gallimard, 1986).
6. Jean-Paul Sartre, *Lettres au Castor et à quelques autres* (Paris: Gallimard, 1983).
7. See Ponge's introduction to *Proèmes* in *Tome premier* (Paris: Gallimard, 1965), p. 109.
8. Madame de Sévigné, *Lettres* (Paris: Garnier Flammarion, 1976), p. 68.
9. Ibid., p. 101.

10. See Jean Starobinski, *Montaigne en mouvement* (Paris: Gallimard, 1962), pp. 52–53.
11. Christian Meurillon, "La lettre au coeur de l'écriture pascalienne," *Revue des sciences humaines,* 195 (1984).

1. Destination: Distance

1. Daniel Oster, *Passages de Zénon* (Paris: Editions du Seuil, 1983), pp. 19–29.
2. Kafka recommended to Felice that she read Flaubert's letters as well as his novels.
3. This is not his practice with everyone. He discusses all his drafts with his friend Louis Bouilhet, who becomes, after others (notably Ernest Chevalier and Alfred Le Poittevin), a sort of alter ego, an ideal confidant in whom he has absolute trust and in whose company he can even work.
4. Alain Buisine, *Proust et ses lettres* (Lille: Presses Universitaires de Lille, 1983), pp. 110–125.
5. Proust is never in synchronicity with anyone else, as Buisine points out. Ibid., pp. 92–99.
6. Rilke's paradoxical visit to Capri in January 1907 is the perfect example. He insists above all on absolute solitude, indispensable to his work, and refuses to mix in society—but he retreats to a fashionable, heavily touristed spot. See B. Böschenstein, "Les lettres de Capri (janvier 1907)," *Europe,* March 1980.
7. "But, oh Dearest! How agreeable I know you to be, that in yesterday's letter you encouraged me, bravely and boldly *to stay!* With those few words, which did not seem too disheartened, you lifted my heart and lowered it again where it lay once more, on the altar where it must burn for a few months longer. Oh, if it were possible for my feeling for you to grow any larger, at that instant I felt in it a fullness such that I had to close my eyes and wrap myself in my own arms (as during that night of which I told you) to contain it. Yes, beloved, help me in this heroic way, mold yourself to this serene landscape, these quiet walls that protect me, protect me with them—be, oh be that fountain which all this time has been insisting: 'stay, stay . . .' I am here, I set the example of that shift you must make within yourself" (to Merline, December 16, 1920). Good old Merline, who not only encourages Rilke to stay where he is and not come to see her, but who will even sacrifice their correspondence and meet him only through a pure shared desire for solitude: "René, you *shouldn't* answer my letters, and I think that in time I will write them without sending them. But for the moment, my too-full soul overflows and it is so sweet to let its contents flow softly towards my beloved" (August 31, 1920; letter written in French). The height of epistolary love would be not even to send the letters they write for each other.

2. What Words Lack

1. See, for example, Jacques Lacan, *Ecrits* (Paris: Editions du Seuil, 1966), pp. 524–525.
2. Philippe Bonnefis, *Mesures de l'ombre* (Lille: Presses Universitaires de Lille, 1987), pp. 113–152.
3. Baudelaire's complaints about his lawyer, a source of dishonor and unhappiness all his life, form one of the most recurrent themes of his correspondence with his mother, whom he constantly blames. But the solutions he proposes are often far more ambiguous than his accusations would seem to imply. Baudelaire and Madame Aupick have a complicitous relationship, an implicit agreement to maintain the status quo with Baudelaire as debtor and his mother as sole creditor. It can be seen, for example, in the surprising proposition (repeated several times) that Charles makes when Ancelle first comes on the scene: "I prefer not to have a fortune anymore and to put myself completely in your hands, rather than subject myself to any judgment whatsoever: the first is still an act of freedom, the other is an attack on my freedom" (Summer 1844).
4. See Freud's *Entwurf einer Psychologie* and the commentary proposed by Jacques Lacan in *L'ethique de la psychanalyse. Le seminaire, livre VII* (Paris: Editions du Seuil, 1986), pp. 27–102.
5. Gilles Deleuze and Felix Guattari, *Kafka: Pour une littérature mineure* (Paris: Editions de Minuit, 1975), pp. 51–52.
6. Later Kafka will write the famous *Brief an den Vater,* a long portrait of himself as an unhappy son, which he will never show to his father; nor to Milena, to whom he repeatedly promises a copy. It is always put off until later, until it's too late or, even worse, until they're in Gmünd: "It would help if you read my (incidentally bad and unnecessary) letter to my father. Maybe I'll take it along to Gmünd" (August 9, 1920). A rendezvous in Gmünd means a rendezvous nowhere, with a letter that would explain a great deal but will never arrive. The letter to his father must never be sent if Kafka is to write and send all his other letters. The Kafkaesque epistolary system is a long and necessarily secret denunciation of his father, the incarnation of a law he must be able to evade. If the secret were told, if the denunciation of his father became a denunciation *to* his father, the whole system would break down, leaving only the bridge from "The Judgment" for Kafka to jump from.
7. Against her will? There is no way of knowing for sure. There has been a lot of speculation about Grete's feelings for Kafka; some think she was very much in love with him. There is also the letter written in 1940 to a friend, in which she claims to have had, around 1915, an illegitimate child who died in Munich in 1921. Who other than Kafka could have been the father? Did she get the date wrong? Was it the result of delirium? She wasn't completely

rational during the period in which the letter was written. Nothing in her letters or in what we know of her life confirms the existence of a child or Kafka's hypothetical fatherhood. But the anecdote is thought-provoking and carries a grain of truth: Kafka could only have been a father in delirious imagination or in absolute secrecy, illegitimate father of an illegitimate child.

8. For more on this double bind, see Gregory Bateson, *Steps to an Ecology of Mind* (San Francisco: Chandler, 1972).

9. Deleuze and Guattari, *Kafka,* pp. 61–62.

10. Not all of Proust's letters are hollow and mundane. The most notable exceptions are those written to his editors (Grasset and especially Jacques Rivière and Gaston Gallimard) during the editing stage of *La recherche*—which give some inkling of his true interests. His sickness may prevent him from fully existing, but it never prevents him from standing up for the language he has made his own, his writing.

11. Stéphane Mallarmé, *Oeuvres complètes* (Paris: Bibliothèque de la Pléiade, Gallimard, 1945), p. 664.

12. Leo Bersani, *The Death of Stéphane Mallarmé* (Cambridge: Cambridge University Press, 1982).

13. Mallarmé, *Oeuvres complètes,* p. 1502.

14. Notably Maurice Blanchot, *Le livre à venir* (Paris: Gallimard, 1959), pp. 53–62, and Laurent Jenny, *La terreur et les signes* (Paris: Gallimard, 1982), pp. 213–217.

15. Jacques Derrida, "La parole soufflée," in *L'écriture et la différence* (Paris: Editions du Seuil, 1967).

16. Artaud, *Oeuvres complètes,* vol. 1, p. 13.

3. Images, Memories, Mourning

1. See Jean-Louis Cornille, *L'amour des lettres ou le contrat déchiré* (Mannheim-Analytiques 3, 1985), pp. 206–235, on the connection between letter writing and photography in Kafka's work.

   Deleuze and Guattari in their *Kafka* speak of the vampire in Kafka's epistolary practices. Kafka paradoxically echoes this by claiming a cloud as his portrait: vampires are traditionally recognized by their inability to cast a reflection in a mirror or on photographic film.

2. Kafka, unlike Felice, did not like to travel but loved hotels. Their ideas on the pleasures of homelife were diametrically opposed.

3. Pierre Pachet, *La force de dormir* (Paris: Gallimard, 1988), pp. 123–142.

4. This kind of association appears earlier, in 1848, in Flaubert's letter to Du Camp on the death of Alfred Le Poittevin, his main confidant: "Now and then I got up, lifted the veil covering his face, and looked at him. I was wrapped in a cloak that belonged to my father and which he had worn only

once, the day of Caroline's wedding" (April 7, 1848). To keep watch over his dead friend, Flaubert wraps himself in his dead father's coat; a coat worn only once, at Caroline's wedding, when Gustave had to give her up for the first time to her husband, Hamard; a coat that Dr. Flaubert did not live to wear again a year later at his daughter's funeral.

5. In 1846 Flaubert predicts that it will take him ten years to recover fully from the death of the woman who was his only audience and to find another to take her place. He is not far wrong: *Madame Bovary* appears in 1856.

6. Jacques Derrida, *La carte postale* (Paris: Aubier-Flammarion, 1980), p. 39.

7. This is also the principal charm of war for Proust: "Since the war I live in fear for all the people I love (even, deep down, for those whom I don't know and whose sufferings I imagine so vividly" (to Robert de Billy, March 1915). Proust is never so busy as during the war; he has never had so much suffering to imagine and sympathize with, countless losses to share and condolence letters to write. War gives him the chance to sympathize with the most anonymous grief; it opens all borders to him. It is an almost infinite enlargement of the imaginary space his letters can inhabit.

8. Is it a coincidence that Proust is forced, several times, to reassure people of the sincerity of his sympathy? That he is sometimes taken for a hypocrite, most notably in the letter to Antoine Bibesco cited above? Eight years later, he takes advantage of the death of the Bibesco brothers' father, to reconsider the disagreement that took place at the time of their mother's death: a misfortune, he writes, "which touched me so profoundly that I can think of it only with pain—and that I would remember sweetly as having allowed me to communicate more completely with you and Emmanuel, if, on the contrary, because of a foul and useless lie which you must have believed since you repeated it to me, it hadn't ended our friendship by preventing me from continuing truly to love those who believed me a hypocrite" (to Antoine Bibesco, August 11, 1911).

9. This could be Proust's true *cogito*: "I suffer, therefore I am." Also, since we are in the realm of reversals, "I cause suffering, therefore I am"—the formula we find in a letter to André Gide, thanking him for having sent *Laf Cadio's Adventures:* "It would take ten letters, or rather ten conversations, to make you understand the pain that Cadio has inflicted on me and that is, first of all, the proof that he exists: 'I cause suffering, therefore I am'" (April 6 or 7, 1914). Suffering makes up Proust's entire philosophy or, more exactly, his credo, his substitute for faith. In a letter in which he describes his lack of religious faith, he adds, "It seems to me that Suffering alone has made and continues to make man into a little bit more than an animal" (to Lionel Hauser, September 1915).

10. Jean-Louis Baudry, *Proust, Freud et l'autre* (Paris: Editions de Minuit, 1984).

11. On this point see Alain Grosrichard, "L'oeil-de-boeuf," forthcoming in *Ornicar?*.

4. The Letter, the Book

1. You don't bury a friend like Mallarmé every day, nor do you meet a soulmate every day. It happens even less often that you bury the friend and meet your future wife on the same day, as Valéry did—he was introduced to Jeannie Gobillard (one of Julie Manet's cousins) at the funeral. It is certainly a day he does not want to forget.

2. See my *Le livre et ses adresses* (Paris: Meridiens-Klincksieck, 1986).

3. Valéry, *Cahiers I* (Paris: Bibliothèque de la Pléiade, Gallimard, 1973), pp. 310–311.

4. Unlike Valéry, Gide engages in several epistolary exchanges at the same time. Robert Mallet, editor of their correspondence, notes one of Gide's more telling remarks on this topic in his introduction: "I made a career of friendship. It is a tiring career that requires a lot of personal care. I wore myself out with it. I wrote little to each, but I wrote a lot" (p. 9). Friendship, for Gide, is one of the duties of a writer.

5. For Rilke, psychoanalysis is closely connected to Lou; Lou's decision to become an analyst may result from her contact with Rilke, an ideal first case. See also Jacques Le Rider's afterword to Lou Andreas-Salomé, *Rainer Maria Rilke* (Paris: Maren Sell, 1989), pp. 111–122. Le Rider concludes that Lou supported Rilke's reluctance to undergo treatment, since she was more interested in witnessing his writing than his therapy. Le Rider also suggests that Lou's *Rilke*, written immediately after his death, was inspired largely by the guilt she felt at not having encouraged him to seek treatment.

6. Rainer Maria Rilke, *The Notebooks of Malte Laurids Brigge*, trans. M. D. Herter Norton (New York: Norton, 1949), p. 66.

7. Ibid., p. 68.

8. Mallarmé, *Oeuvres complètes*, p. 372.

9. Albert Rombaud, "Destination: inconnu," *Revue des sciences humaines*, 195 (1984).

10. Flaubert to Louise: "An author in his book must be like God in the universe, present everywhere and visible nowhere. Art being a second Nature, the creator of that Nature must behave similarly. In all its atoms, in all its aspects, let there be sensed a hidden, infinite impassivity" (December 9, 1852).

11. Works addressed to no one in particular, or even to a missing person, whose fundamental role is to be missing—this could be Lacan's barred Other, the absence that supports desire. The epistolary turns against the Other, as representative of the law, in favor of the barred Other and the reinvention of speech and desire. See Marie-Christine Hamon, "De la correspondance," *Ornicar?* 36 (1985).

12. There have been contradictory interpretations of the fragments published by J. Scherer. Some consider them the outline for Mallarmé's ultimate polyphonic work; others find them proof of its failure and impossibility. I read

the fragments as a *speculation* on belief in the Book. Mallarmé's notes seem intended to inspire the debate. See *Le livre et ses adresses.*

13. Maurice Pujo (1872–1955) later helped found Action française and managed its magazine from 1917 to 1943. Judging by the evidence, he was not impressed by the policy of "limited action" that Mallarmé advocated. But, then, it is harder to believe in limited action than in *action française.*

14. The numerous thank-you letters Mallarmé wrote in return for books, poems, dedications, and so on, are worth closer study. First of all, toward the end of his life they take up a considerable part of his correspondence; it is almost as if he writes only to say thank you. Second, his thanks, always so kind on the surface, are sometimes more ironic than they seem. Even in his most insignificant or coded acts, Mallarmé remains the prince of ambiguity: he allows his correspondents to read into his letters whatever they most want to hear, confirming their faith, time after time, in their own beliefs. Finally, these letters are often stylistically surprising. They seem to be rough drafts for a style Mallarmé will realize most fully in collections such as *Crayonné au théâtre* or *Variations sur un sujet.* Like other writers, Mallarmé gains access to literature through his letters—a hypothesis that does not contradict my earlier conclusions if we bear in mind that Mallarmé's "critical poems" are constantly questioning the existence of the poetic and, consequently, of the Book. Some of the *Variations,* in fact, openly demonstrate that the Book is both everywhere and nowhere. Though letters provide Mallarmé with another entry into writing, it is a form of writing that works toward the dissolution of literature as we know it.

15. Such an approach to Artaud's madness should allow us at least to avoid the old debate about the coherence of his works. There is nothing in his writing that cannot be understood in one way or another, with a little good will and energy on the part of the reader. This is not to imply that his madness was imagined—there is nothing more coherent than delirium. By situating Artaud's madness in his efforts to take literature literally, rather than in the context or body of his actions, we also avoid harping on the tired themes of writing and madness, which have been endlessly discussed in avant-garde theory texts. The equivalence of the two is entirely metaphorical: it may be convenient to believe that writing is always linked to madness, but madness, in this context, remains only an image or idea—it is never taken literally.

Index

Index